The Traditions

of

Ingersley Hall

Bridget J Franklin

Published 2016 by Bridget Jane Franklin

16 Millers Meadow
Rainow
Macclesfield
Cheshire
SK10 5UE

Copyright © Bridget Franklin 2016

ISBN 978-1-5262-0439-4

All rights reserved. No part of this publication may be reproduced, stored in a retrieval system, or transmitted, in any form or by any means, without the prior permission in writing of the author and publisher.

Printed by: Printdomain

Cover illustration: White Nancy c1910, by permission of Bollington Civic Society.
Background: extract from plan of Ingersley estate produced for the auction in 1933.
Back cover illustration: Front elevation of Ingersley Hall, photograph by the author.

Contents

	Acknowledgements	2
	Foreword	3
	Family Tree	5
1.	The Early Days	7
2.	Land and Inheritance	13
3.	The Move to Ingersley	23
4.	A New Generation at Ingersley	31
5.	The Life of a Country Squire	38
6.	The Last Gaskell at Ingersley	52
7.	After the Gaskells	57
	Notes and References	64

Acknowledgements

A number of individuals and organisations have been invaluable in assisting with the research for this book. I am particularly indebted to Tom Swailes who has directed me to a number of historical sources, and with whom I have had various helpful discussions about the Gaskells and Ingersley. The following have also offered information or assistance: Bob Langstaff, Fiona Swailes, David Williams, Richard Gaskell, the Salesians of Savio House, Bollington Discovery Centre, Rainow History Group, Cheshire Record Office, Greater Manchester County Record Office, John Rylands Library, and Macclesfield Library.

With the exception of those credited below, the black and white photographs in the text are reproduced from the archive collections of Rainow Image Library and Bollington Civic Society, with their kind permission. The illustration of Lyme Hall is from J.P. Neale and T. Moule (1819) *Jones' Views of the Seats of Noblemen and Gentlemen*, Sherwood, Neely and Jones. The portrait of Thomas Gaskell is in the possession of John Shaw's Club, Manchester, and is reproduced in F.S. Stancliffe (1938) *John Shaw's 1738- 1938*, Sherratt and Hughes. The map of Ingersley is from a 1907 Ordnance Survey map and is included courtesy of Alan Godfrey Maps. The pictures of Errwood Hall and of the group which includes John Francis Gaskell are taken from the website *www.goyt-valley.org.uk* by permission of David Stirling. The coloured plan showing the division into lots of the Ingersley estate is drawn from the details of the auction sale in 1933, with thanks to the Salesians and Tom Swailes. The photograph of the Orford memorial tablet, the boundary stone and all colour photographs are by the author.

Foreword

Four years ago I joined a small group of people working together in the walled garden of the former Ingersley Hall, now known as Savio House. This was once at the centre of a sizeable estate and is situated on the fringe of the village of Rainow in the Pennine foothills of east Cheshire. The family who came to live here some 250 years ago were called Gaskell, but upon investigation it seemed there was very little readily available information about them: who they were; where they had come from; how they lived; and what happened to them. I therefore decided to research them myself, and this short book is a result of that research.

It has not been an easy task. The Gaskells who lived at Ingersley Hall were neither famous nor eminent, and were not, for example, aristocrats, MPs, major industrialists or reformers (nor were they related to the Mrs Elizabeth Gaskell of literary fame). This means that there is scant material in the public domain, and a further complication is the historic proliferation of people in Cheshire with the name Gaskell, especially between the seventeenth and nineteenth centuries. Many of these Gaskells also bore the same first names, both within and between generations, so disentangling them has taken many laborious hours. It is hardly surprising then that there has been some confusion about the family trees of the different branches of the Gaskells, or that this confusion has been reproduced over time.

In regard to the Ingersley Gaskells this has led in particular to the conflation of the identity of two different but contemporaneous Thomas Gaskells. One is the childless Thomas Gaskell, fustian merchant of Manchester and President of the Shaw Club, who never lived at Ingersley. The other is his nephew, who predeceased his uncle by three years, and who inherited Ingersley and was the father of the better known John Upton Gaskell.

Whilst it has thus been possible to trace the names and dates of the Ingersley Gaskells and the relationships between them, it is not so easy to provide a rounded picture of their lives and their characteristics, particularly for the early generations. This is due to the very limited information that exists and the fact that the Gaskells themselves disposed of many of their family papers and photographs in the early part of the twentieth century. Reference is necessarily made to many different people and places, and hopefully this is not too bemusing to the reader. A family tree is included in order to give some clarity to the relationships between the central characters.

The first two chapters of this book cover the period before the Gaskells came to Ingersley. These chapters show how, from humble beginnings as tenants of the Leghs of Lyme, the Gaskells rose in status to become members of the landed gentry and possessors of several estates. This they achieved through astute investment in land

and through the happenstance of a degree of childlessness. Together with some judicious marriages, this led to the concentration of wealth in fewer hands than might otherwise have been the case.

The next four chapters concern the four generations of Gaskells who lived at Ingersley Hall, involving a total period of some 150 years. Included is the story of the building of the prominent monument 'White Nancy', illustrated on the front cover. Finally, some attention is given to the time after the Gaskells left, when, following a sale and a fire, Ingersley received a new incarnation as Savio House.

Family Tree of the Gaskells
(main Ingersley line highlighted)

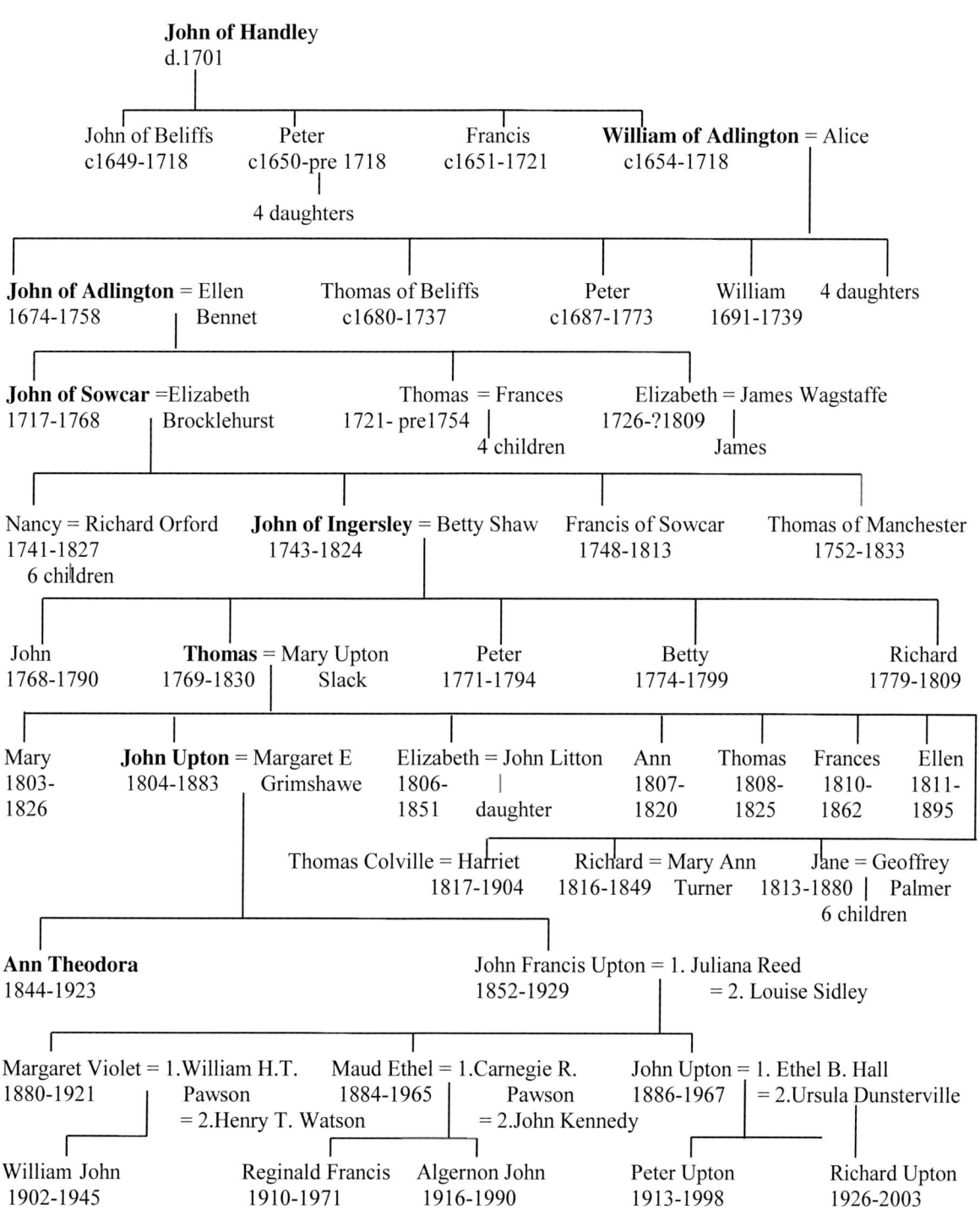

1. The Early Days

The earliest ancestors of the Gaskells of Ingersley are likely to have come from what is now Cumbria, created from the amalgamation of the old counties of Cumberland and Westmorland. Here there are two small settlements, one named Gatesgill, also spelt Gaitsgill, south of Carlisle, and the other named Gaisgill, east of Tebay. The first recording of Gatesgill was as Geytescales in 1273 but subsequently there were a number of other broadly phonetic spellings such as Gaytscale and Gaytschales.[1] When surnames were first introduced in the fourteenth century, these place names, like so many others, were used as the basis for what eventually became patronyms handed on down the generations. Thus it is possible to find the early recording of names such as Benjamin de Gaytscale, William de Gaytscale and Simon de Gaytscales; and Alicia de Gasegill, Agnes de Gasegyll, and Johanes de Gaysegill. It is the descendants of these people who bear today the name Gaskell, together with its variants of Gaitskill, Gaitskell, Gaskill and Gaskall.[2]

It would seem that some of the early Gaskells migrated southwards from the old Cumbrian counties, possibly after the Black Death of 1348 and 1349. Before then, most tenants had effectively been bound by the rigid feudal system, subject to their masters and not able to move elsewhere. However, the deaths of so many people meant that landowners were desperate for workers and were forced to offer more favourable types of tenancy. Thus individuals were freer to move about the country to seek new opportunities and better living conditions. Certainly by the fourteenth century there were Gaskells in Lancashire, and indeed Lancashire became a stronghold of Gaskells, as it still is today.

By the sixteenth and early seventeenth centuries there were Gaskells recorded in Cheshire. The earliest such reference is to Gaskells as tenants of the Leghs of Lyme in the 16th century (see below), whilst in the 1611 survey of Macclesfield Manor and Forest there were a handful of Gaskells recorded in Pott Shrigley and Kettleshulme. Into the 17th century and beyond there were Gaskells to be found in some numbers in the contiguous townships of Lyme Handley, Pott Shrigley, Disley, Harrop, Rainow, Kettleshulme, Bollington and Adlington. By contrast to the situation in Lancashire, however, there are very few Gaskells in these places today.

The Gaskells who later came to Ingersley were descended from Gaskells living in Lyme Handley, an upland area on the north-eastern fringe of Cheshire in the Pennine hills. Historically most of the township of Lyme Handley lay within the royal forest of Macclesfield, which at the time was vastly larger than the Macclesfield Forest of today. It was owned by the king who used it primarily for hunting, but also developed a few areas for cattle pasturage, including one within Lyme Handley. In 1398 most of the land of Lyme Handley was granted by Richard II to Piers Legh (1360-1399), son of Robert Legh of Adlington (1308-1370) for services rendered.[3]

Initially the Leghs had no permanent residence there as they continued to live on their main estates in Lancashire, but they did maintain a hunting lodge as a base from which to lead hunting parties. In about 1450 a more substantial house was built at Lyme, and this was then refashioned a hundred years later when the Leghs decided to make it their main home.[4] It would seem a not unreasonable proposition that after the Leghs had begun to develop the estate and its capacities, and given the lack of local populace, they might have brought over from Lancashire people they could trust to manage the land. This then might have included one or more Gaskells - known to be in Lancashire at the time - and it is a matter of record that there was some movement of personnel between the various Legh estates.

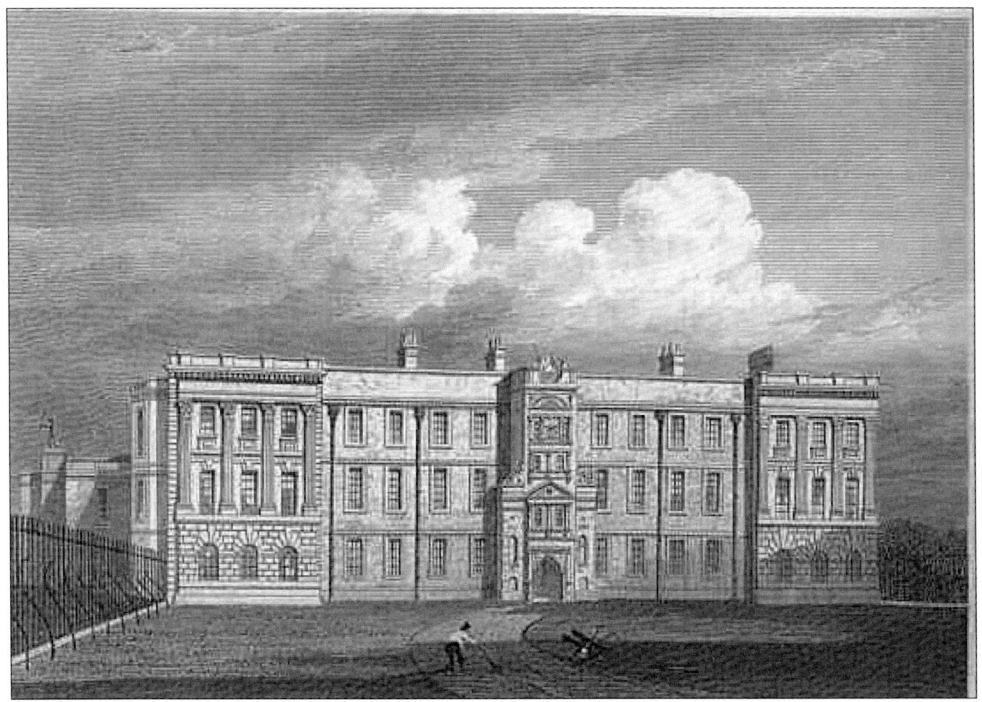

Lyme Hall in the early 19th Century

Research indicates that in the fourteenth century there were no Gaskells in either Lyme Handley or the larger area of Macclesfield Forest.[5] In the following century, in 1466, a survey was carried out covering the whole of Peter Legh's holdings.[6] On the Lyme estate (which covered most of the township of Lyme Handley) there were only 11 'messuages' (dwellings) and whilst the names of the tenants were listed none of them were Gaskells. This does not, however, preclude the possibility that there might have been Gaskells as sub-tenants, or as servants living in accommodation within the Legh's own property. Over the next 50 years or so the number of messuages increased to 35, although unfortunately no names of tenants are recorded for this period.[7]

However there is other evidence that by the early 1500s there were a handful of Gaskells living in Lyme Handley. This derives from the parish records of baptisms, marriages and burials, which were required to be kept from 1538. Lyme Handley lay in the large parish of Prestbury and was served by the church of St Peter's, but many records are also to be found at the church of St Mary's, Disley, which was built by the Leghs and geographically closer. Occasionally the churches at Pott Shrigley or Taxal were also used. The earliest Lyme Handley record relating to a Gaskell is the marriage of Peter Gaskell in 1561. This is followed by the marriages of Thomasyn, Ayme and Ellen around 1590. The earliest burial is of Renold Gaskell in 1592, and the earliest baptism is of Anne Gaskell in 1605. Numbers of Gaskells recorded in this way slowly increase over time, as one might expect.[8]

The Church of St Peter's Prestbury, where many of the Gaskells were baptised, married and buried

There are also some sixteenth century records relating more specifically to Gaskells as tenants and servants of the Leghs. The first of these occurs in two Court of Star Chamber cases dated 1538 and 1540.[9] In the first case there were complaints that Piers Legh and some of his tenants, including Reynold Gatstathe and William Gaitschayle (also referred to in the same document as Gatstathe and Gaskells, in the typically idiosyncratic and non-standardised spelling of the time), had unlawfully brought their cattle on to a common that was the King's land. In the second case, dated 1540, Reygnold Gaitschale of Hanley, husbandman, 'farmer unto Leigh' (also referred to as Reignold Getstathe, Gaitscayle and Gayscaley), was named as being involved in similar cases.[10] The spellings Gaitschayle and Gaitscayle lend credence to the idea that these Gaskells had originated in Gatesgill, formerly Geytescales or Gaitschayle, as noted above.

Further early Gaskells are named in other documents relating to the Leghs. A Lyme account book of 1607 refers to the expenses of John Gaiskell when he took sheep to market and horses to Warrington fair.[11] There are also a few letters that survive from this same period. One letter, written in the early 1600s, is from Francis Gaskell of 'Lime' to Peter Legh, referring to beasts and their price at a sale, and to the need for servants. This could perhaps be from a steward or bailiff, and ends: 'Your servant to command Ffrancis Gaskell'. There is also a letter from Peter Legh to Peter Gaskell at Lyme, of a similar date, requesting him to kill a buck and present it to 'my Lord Bishop'.[12]

Another reference to Gaskells occurs in the context of the funeral procession of Peter Legh in 1636 from his home in Lyme to his burial place in Winwick, Lancashire, some 30 miles distant. The procession was said to consist of several hundred people and many are mentioned by name, including Robert Gasceyll, Francis Gasceyll and Piers (Peter) Gasceyll (presumably the latter two are the same as in the letters above). These names are not subsumed into the general category of 'tenants', as if they are of superior rank, yet below the rank of 'gentlemen' whose names are prefixed with 'Mr'.

The name Francis appears for a third time in 1646 in an inventory in which Francis Gaskell, yeoman of Lyme Handley, had livestock and possessions to the value of over £150, a not inconsiderable amount at the time, with the letters of administration being granted to John Gaskell, probably a son or brother. John was the most common first name current both at the time and for the next several hundred years, and locally Peter was not unusual, in deference to the many generations of Peter Leghs at Lyme. The name Francis however was uncommon, and it is interesting to note that Francis has been in use by the Ingersley Gaskells down the generations from at least the mid seventeenth century until the present day. Thus it seems a strong possibility that the Francis mentioned in the above mentioned documents, assuming they are all the same person, could be an Ingersley forebear.

In 1686 a new survey was carried out by Richard Legh, the then owner of Lyme.[13] This shows that there were then 33 messuages, and of these six were occupied by Gaskells as tenants of the Leghs:

John Gaskils of Bolinhurst, 174 acres;
John Geskils of Beliffs, 112 acres;
Peter Gaskils of The Hagg (also known as Haighe), 62 acres;
John Gaskils of Cornfield, 49 acres;
Thomas Gaskils (probably of Lower Cliffe, near Kettleshulme), 36 acres;
Gaskills of Rilswood (now Ryles Wood, south of High Lane), 42 acres.

It seems probable that all these Gaskells were related, although it has not proved possible to trace the precise nature of the relationships. There was, however, a definite connection between the Gaskells of Beliffs, The Hagg (a tannery), and Cornfield, and the occupants of these were probably all descended from one person who lived in the mid or early sixteenth century. But what is clear from information in wills and other sources, is that Beliffs was a former home of the Ingersley Gaskells. This is now known as Baileys Farm, and lies a mile or so from the eastern boundary of today's Lyme Park.

Baileys Farm, formerly Beliffs, home of early Gaskells in Lyme Handley

Thus the picture is that from the early 1500s and possibly before, there are a number of Gaskells living as tenants of the Leghs, some with a large acreage and the status of yeoman, some as husbandmen, and some as servants, stockmen or bailiffs. Given the limited number of positions and the lack of available tenancies (in 1810 there were still only 35 messuages on the Leghs' extensive land) it would not have been possible for all the offspring of the fairly prolific Gaskell families to have found occupation in Lyme Handley. This explains why many had to move away, and accounts for the gradual increase in numbers in the surrounding townships.

Amongst those who sought new land and opportunity were the Ingersley Gaskells, although it took a few generations and a number of steps before the land at Ingersley was acquired.

2. Land and Inheritance

The first directly traceable forebear of the Ingersley Gaskells is John of Handley who died in 1701. His wife was probably named Aimee, and she died in 1663 after the birth of their last child Thomas. Both John and Aimee were buried at the church of St Mary's in Disley. Thomas, along with two others, did not live beyond infancy, but there were four surviving sons: John, Francis, Peter and William. John of Handley almost certainly lived at Beliffs and was fairly well to do for the time, with at his death 13 head of cattle and goods valued at over £169. His grandchildren as well as his sons were left money and other items in his will, one of these being a coffer (chest) engraved with a J and G, bequeathed to his grandson John. As all eldest sons of the Ingersley line were named John up until the twentieth century, it is possible John of Handley's father was also John, but it is not possible to confirm this, especially given the fact that there were several John Gaskells at the time in Lyme Handley.

John and his young sons lived through some of the most turbulent times in English history, witnessing the civil war, the establishment of the Protectorate under Oliver Cromwell, the restoration of the monarchy, the Great Plague (which reached the local area), and the banishment of James II when William and Mary took the throne in 1688. The Leghs were noted royalists and Jacobites, receiving the Duke of York, later James II, as a visitor, and they were also believed to be Catholic sympathisers at a time of religious upheaval and intolerance. One consequence of this was that, like other people in official and trusted positions, they had to swear allegiance to the Church of England and the Crown. Richard Legh MP (1634-1687), the then owner of Lyme, was one who had to comply with this decree, and it could well be John Gaskell of Handley, Ingersley forebear, who was the John Gaskell of Hanley, yeoman, who witnessed a sacrament certificate for him at the church in Disley on 25 December 1684.[14]

The four sons of John of Handley lived to see more prosperous and stable times and it was through them that wealth and property began to be accrued. The oldest son was John (c1649-1718) who had no children. The second son Peter (c1650-pre 1718) was a tanner, perhaps learning his trade from relatives at the Hagg. Tanning at the time could be a lucrative (as well as a noxious) business, as leather was much in demand for everything from saddlery and harnesses, gloves and shoes, to bellows and book bindings, and he eventually acquired Bank Hall near Chapel-en-le-Frith. He had four daughters but no sons. The third son of John of Handley, Francis (c1651-1721) was apparently unmarried and certainly had no children, and the fourth son, William (c1654-1718), was the Ingersley forebear.

Both John and Francis were successful yeomen and investors in land. John acquired property in Marple and Kettleshulme as well as a larger holding in Nightwigg in the parish of Glossop (also known as Knightwigg or Knightwick, and today as Knightwake Farm on the north-west edge of New Mills). His brother Francis acquired a sizeable estate in Ollerenshaw, near Chapel-en-le-Frith in 1697, although neither he nor his heirs lived there. They both left considerable assets in their wills; John over £760, and Francis the impressive amount of £1532. Francis clearly also had a philanthropic tendency as his bequests included a number of charitable donations to the poor. As neither John nor Francis had children it was their youngest brother William and his children who were the eventual beneficiaries.

William, as the youngest son with fewer opportunities, was the one of the four brothers who moved away from Handley. This occurred in the early 1690s after the birth of most of his eight children, and the place he moved to was Longdoles in Adlington. Longdoles consisted of land with two farms, Higher Doles and Lower Doles, and lay to the north of Whiteley Green bordering Sugar Lane.[15] Lower Doles is today a cottage whilst the larger Higher Doles farmhouse is a listed building of early seventeenth century origin with some mullioned windows and sliding sashes. The land at Longdoles was owned by the Leghs of Adlington, distant cousins of the Leghs of Lyme. It is not clear what led William to settle here, other than that at the time the Adlington Leghs were beginning to enclose more land and needed reliable tenants. William may also have been a tanner, especially as two of his sons were tanners.

Higher Longdoles today, original house on the right with mullioned windows.

William became known as William of Adlington, and of the eight children by his wife Alice, four were daughters and four were sons. His four daughters were Joan, Ann, Mary and Amy, who married respectively John Lucas, Henry Royle, James Judson, and Ralph Leah. His two older sons were John (c1674-1758) and Thomas (c1680-1737), and it was his two younger sons who became tanners: William the younger (c1691-1739) stayed in Adlington; and Peter (c1689-1773) later had a tannery on what was at the time Legh land on the River Dean in Bollington near the site of the later Waterhouse Mill. He eventually moved to Bollington Cross. Neither of these two had children, so the beneficiaries of their wills were their older brothers John and Thomas, together with John's three children. Although William the younger died at a relatively early age he had assets of over £1000 (including £66 worth of bark and leather 'wet and dry'), and like his uncle Francis he left money to the poor. He is buried in the same grave as his father William and brother Peter, together with Peter's wife, in the churchyard at Prestbury.

Thomas, William of Adlington's second son, lived with his childless uncle John at Beliffs in Handley, a decision made perhaps to improve his chances in life. He followed the example of land acquisition established by his two uncles, and turned his attention to the Rainow area, where shortly before his death in 1737 he acquired Laneside (on Blaze Hill), land in nearby Hedgerow, and the farm Sowcar (pronounced Sooca) on the Bollington border. The large farmhouse here still stands opposite the entrance to Ingersley Hall, and is a listed building dating from Elizabethan times, although it is believed there was a building on the site for several hundred years prior to that. Thomas never married and had no children, so again his assets passed to his brothers and to the children of his oldest brother John. Having inherited Beliffs he left it to his two unmarried cousins Mary and Elizabeth, who had lived with him at Beliffs. Thomas too, gave sums to benefit the poor, and also 2d (two pennies in pre-decimal currency) to each poor person who attended his funeral.

It was William of Adlington's first born son, known as John of Adlington, who first acquired land at Ingersley. At first glance his prospects would seem not particularly favourable: his father had been a youngest son with few assets and a large family; one of his brothers had gone to live with an uncle; and the two others had had to turn to tanning. However the situation for John was vastly improved due to the fact that several of his relatives had prospered and, more importantly, had no children of their own. So whilst John succeeded to his father's tenancy of Longdoles where he made his home, he also inherited through his uncle Francis the large estate of Ollerenshaw, had an interest through his brother Peter in Nightwigg, and received monetary legacies from his grandfather, uncles and brothers. Thus as he grew older he was in a more secure position, and looking to invest in further assets. It may be through his brother Thomas' acquisition of the land at Sowcar, Hedgerow and Laneside that his attention was drawn to the adjacent Ingersley, especially as Thomas had left all of these to John's own son, also known as John. There was in addition an element of serendipity at work.

Sowcar Farm c1900

At the time Ingersley was owned by the Downes of Shrigley Hall, major landowners in the area, but in the early 1700s they had built up crippling debts and were seeking to raise loans. They therefore mortgaged considerable amounts of land, including Ingersley and the neighbouring Lima Farm, to John Brocklehurst (1718-1796) (whose family had been in the area since at least the fourteenth century and who later founded the famous Macclesfield silk mill and a local bank). Another factor in the equation was that John of Adlington's son John was betrothed to the above John Brocklehurst's first cousin Elizabeth, whose father was also called John Brocklehurst (1668-1757), and who resided at Tower Hill in Rainow. Clearly the situation was extremely complicated (and requires a legal expert to unravel), but it would seem that the Brocklehursts allowed possession of the land to pass to John of Adlington, perhaps connected with the marriage settlement of 1738, even though the Downes were still the legal owners.[16] Ingersley was in fact a particularly beneficial acquisition as it had been a thriving concern from the seventeenth century and before, with good quality land and the largest cattle herd in Rainow.[17]

John of Adlington did not himself live at Ingersley, but remained at Longdoles. Here he had three children by his wife Ellen Bennet of Reddish Farm in Taxal, who died in 1730. In addition to the oldest son, John, there was Thomas, who died in his early 30s leaving a widow Frances (née Johnson) and four small children, and Elizabeth, who married James Wagstaff.

John of Adlington died in 1758 at the age of 84 and was buried alongside his father, William of Adlington, and his brother, William, at Prestbury. John had been accorded the rank of yeoman and appears to have been extremely well respected, being frequently named as an executor of wills (including that of Peter Gaskell of Hagg who called him 'my affectionate kinsman'), and being a trustee for charitable activities. His will took six years to prove, partly because it was extremely complicated but probably also because of the uncertain status of the Ingersley estate.

He left much of his property, by now including Waulk Mill, the site of the old fulling mill in Rainow adjacent to Ingersley, to his son John. There were, however, various clauses and caveats relating to his brother Peter, and to provision for the children of his deceased son Thomas. He also warned that if anyone is 'discontented' with their legacies and takes any action that is 'litigious or troublesome' to the executors or other legatees, then they will forfeit their legacy and get nothing but five shillings. As regards his prized personal effects, his son John was to have the coffer (chest) engraved with a J and a G that had been passed down from John of Handley, as well as a pistol, a hand cane, a silver tobacco box (also engraved JG), and a great Bible with two brass clasps.[18] Again, charitable sums were left, in this case to the 'poor housekeepers' of Adlington, and half a guinea to the Vicar of Prestbury.

John of Adlington's oldest son John (1717-1768) was initially known as John of Adlington the Younger, but later became referred to as John of Sowcar. He was 40 when his father died in 1758 and only outlived him by 10 years. Even before his father's death he had property, having inherited the Moors in Marple from his childless uncle William, and, as noted above, Sowcar, Hedgerow and Laneside from his equally childless uncle Thomas in 1737. This was fortuitous as it meant that after his marriage in 1738 he could take his bride Elizabeth Brocklehurst to live at Sowcar, suitably upgraded with a new wing. Elizabeth's father John Brocklehurst died in 1757 and having only two daughters, the Gaskells and their children were major beneficiaries. Thus they secured John Brocklehurst's estate of Tower Hill in Rainow which, like Sowcar, is listed and dates from Elizabethan times.

Ten years later, under the terms of his own father's will, John of Sowcar acquired not only the estates of Nightwigg, Longdoles in Adlington, and Ollerenshaw but also Ingersley and Waulk Mill, the ongoing use of which he would secure after paying a sum of money to his Brocklehurst father-in-law's estate. From all these properties and their land he would have received a considerable amount in rent from sub tenants, even though in most cases they were still held copyhold (ie not freehold).[19] This allowed him to acquire further property, notably in 1754 Orme's Tenement, which included Orme's Smithy, and land at Spewley (now Spuley), both situated adjacent to Sowcar and Ingersley on the Pott Shrigley border. In acquiring the land at Spewley, John of Sowcar also had the right to extract coal. This venture must have proved reasonably successful as in his will he directs his executors to continue working all his coal mines with the profits in trust to benefit his younger children. Given that he refers to 'all' his mines, it is probable that this included the small coal mines situated on the Gaskell land at Longdoles, traces of which are still visible today between the former railway (opened in 1869), and the canal (opened in 1831).

John of Sowcar's tombstone in Prestbury churchyard bears witness to the fact that he was the first Gaskell to rise from the rank of yeoman to that of 'gentleman'. This indicated increasing wealth and status, and assured the same rank for his sons as well as an increased eligibility for his daughter. This daughter was Nancy (1741-1827), whilst his sons were John (1743-1824), Francis (1748-1813) and Thomas (1752-1833). Nancy was married in 1767, only nine months before her father's death, to Richard Orford (1733-1791).

Tombstone of John of Sowcar and his wife Elizabeth. St Peter's Prestbury

Richard Orford was the son of John Orford who was a yeoman tenant of Peter Legh of Lyme on his Runcorn estate on the west side of Cheshire. Richard must have caught the eye of the Leghs in some way as in 1760 he was made steward at Lyme, an important position which involved running most of the Leghs' financial and business affairs throughout their several estates. Over the years he rose to be an extremely important figure and amassed considerable wealth and power: 'He developed the coal mines, managed the estates, made most of the deals over land and coal contracts and became more respected than his master'.[20] He and Nancy lived at what became known as Orford House in How Lane, now High Lane, near Disley, where Peter Legh had bequeathed him land in recognition of his services. He was buried in the church on the Legh's estate at Winwick in Lancashire, in itself quite an honour as it was the family burial place of the Leghs, and memorial tablets were placed in the three churches with which he had been associated: Winwick, Disley, and Prestbury. These tablets celebrate the lives not only of Richard, but also of his wife Nancy, their six children, and two of his wife's three Gaskell brothers, all of whom were buried at Prestbury. It is notable that the name of Nancy's eldest brother John, who died in 1824, is not included. This might indicate a lack of closeness between John and his siblings, or it could simply be that whoever erected the plaque, probably an Orford, assumed that John or his children would see to a memorial.

John, the first born son of John of Sowcar, was the beneficiary of much of his father's property. This included the land at Ingersley, although it would appear his father had never paid the amount owed to the Brocklehursts for taking over possession. In 1767 John married Betty Shaw (1740-1818), whose sister Catherine was married to William Clayton (1761-1835). The Claytons had collieries in Poynton and at Swanscoe, and it was William and Catherine's son, also William (1783-1850), who bought the Endon quarries in Kerridge and built both Endon Hall and Endon House (which we will meet again). Initially John and Betty lived at Tower Hill, inherited from the Brocklehursts, but soon after 1775 they and their five children made the move to Ingersley, as discussed further below.

The second son of John of Sowcar, Francis, was only 20 when his father died, and he succeeded to Sowcar. There is no evidence he married and he had no children. Little is known about Francis other than that in 1802 Sowcar Mill was built either on or adjacent to his land, and two years later Francis agreed to the construction of a dam to work the water wheel.[21] This mill was eventually destroyed by fire in 1841 and not rebuilt. Like his father, Francis too described himself as a gentleman and in his will he left his estate and effects equally between his three siblings.

The third son, Thomas, took a rather different direction to the rest of his family. Thomas was only 16 when his father died in 1768 and by the terms of his father's will he could come into his inheritance of Longdoles and Spewley only after his mother's death. His brother John and brother-in-law Richard Orford were named as his guardians until he came of age, and it seems that they, or one of them, arranged for him to start in business as a cotton merchant. Certainly before the age of 21 he was living in Manchester, as confirmed by ongoing correspondence with Richard Orford dating from 1775.

The 90 surviving letters from Thomas are generally very brief and business like, referring mostly to bills of exchange and the need for cash.[22] It would appear Richard Orford was providing something of a banking service; as indeed did many trusted and suitably qualified individuals at a time when the only formal banking system was that

Memorial tablet to the Orfords and to Francis and Thomas Gaskell, St Peter's Prestbury

to be found in London. There is occasional mention of Thomas' business with references to cotton, nankeen, worsted and corduroy, and some indication that samples of materials were provided to the Leghs. It would also appear that initially Thomas was not too successful in his business as he complains about shortage of funds, saying in a rare note of wry humour: 'Poverty again begins to peep in at the windows'.

On one occasion he sent Richard Orford a pair of breeches, as he was a man of 'distinguished taste', and on another some new patterns of cotton which 'are quite the rage'. But personal matters and family rarely feature, with only an occasional passing reference to 'Brother John' (who on one occasion had visited Thomas in Manchester), or to one of Richard's own family. Indeed Thomas seems more exercised about his horse than other people, complaining that the horse suffers frequently from distemper and asking Richard to loan him a mare.

Although Thomas's early days in business may have been a struggle he eventually became a well-respected and very successful fustian merchant. Initially his premises were in Chapel Walks in central Manchester, then later round the corner at 9 Pall Mall, whilst his home was in Piccadilly. He also gained distinction for his Presidency of the Shaw Club, which lasted from 1824 to his death in 1833 at the age of 81. The Shaw Club, strictly speaking the John Shaw Club, had been set up in 1738 and over the years met in a series of different public houses in Manchester. The purpose was to provide a place where the city's more well-to-do Tory merchants could meet to drink punch, toast the King, and discuss the matters of the day. Thomas was first elected at the age of 21 and was thus one of the longest serving members. An idea as to his somewhat portly appearance can be found in the accompanying illustration, taken from an oil painting commissioned by the Shaw Club to celebrate his Presidency.

The Club recorded Thomas' death as follows:

The Club has this year the painful and melancholy duty to record the death of its venerable President Thomas Gaskell, Esq, which took place in Piccadilly on the 8th December this year. He was in the 82nd year of his life, and had been a member of this club for sixty years. He was a constant, daily attendant upon its meetings; and, although he was very lame, from an accident, for many years previous to his death, that circumstance did not prevent his attendance; for when no longer able to walk, he invariably came and returned in a coach. It may with truth be said of him that he was steady and sincere in his friendships, possessed of the most unflinching principles of integrity and the strictest honour and had the esteem of all who had the pleasure to know him.[23]

Thomas had clearly won respect and admiration during the course of his life, and moreover had achieved the rank of Esquire, a step up from gentleman. But he never married and had no children, and this probably accounts for his closeness to his sister Nancy and her family. Indeed, he was also buried in the same grave as his sister and four of her six children in the churchyard at Prestbury. He did not leave a formal will and all that could be found was a handwritten document dated 1820, 13 years before his death.[24] Witnesses had to be found to swear in a court hearing that it was indeed his handwriting. He gave to his nephew Thomas of Tower Hill, son of his older brother John, the estate called Spewley and his interest in Longdoles. Thomas however had predeceased him (in 1830), so it would go to the next in line. The bulk of his estate, worth the significant sum of some £30,000, went to his nephews and nieces by his sister Nancy Orford. One would imagine the Gaskells were not much enamoured of this disposition of his assets, especially as Richard Orford had also been wealthy.

Portrait of Thomas Gaskell of Manchester (1752-1833).

3. The Move to Ingersley

In 1774 John Gaskell, son of John of Sowcar, acquired Ingersley and Lima Farm from the Downes. The Downes had never been in a position to pay off the mortgage they had taken from John Brocklehurst, and the latter agreed to the sale (legally 'conveyance of the fee simple') to John Gaskell even though it was contrary to the still existing rules of the manor and forest of Macclesfield. John Gaskell then proceeded to build for himself a family home in the vicinity of the existing farmhouse. This was not at the time a particularly grand house, consisting of three bays only, but with the plain and elegant Georgian frontage, pleasing proportions, and sash windows that were in favour at the time. It was known as Ingersley House.

Access was gained not at the point of today's driveway from Ingersley Road in Bollington, but from what is now the bridle path called Oakenbank Lane, at the time an important route of ancient origin.[25] From Oakenbank Lane it is possible to see the traces of two different access points, both marked with gateways and stone pillars, and at least one of which predates the building of Ingersley House. The first is on the Rainow side with a gateway opening on to a track over a field. This is the line of a much older route which still exists as a footpath leading down to a probably ancient bridge, later improved by the Gaskells, and on to Ingersley Clough and Waulkmill. From near Oakenbank Lane a track curved off this route towards the house, but the line of this was subsequently blocked by field enclosures. The second approach is nearer the Bollington end and is still visible as a 'causeway' across the parkland, leading through gates over the present drive into Ingersley Clough at the former Ingersley Vale Mill. Again there would have been a spur leading up to the house. The later driveway and entrance from Ingersley Road directly into Bollington was added later, probably in the latter part of the 1820s at the time when Bollington was expanding.

After the house was built, John brought his family to live at Ingersley. It must have been a proud moment; the first house the Gaskells had designed and built, and surrounded by land they called their own. However, the initial euphoria was soon marred by tragedy. Of the five children of John and his wife Betty, four died as young adults. The first son, John, born soon after his parent's marriage, died in 1790 at the age of 22. The third son, Peter, died in 1794, also at the age of 22. The first and only daughter, Betty, named for her mother, died in 1799 aged 24. The fourth son, Richard, died in 1809 at the age of 30. Only the second son, Thomas, survived. It is not known what caused the deaths, this being at a time before death certificates. However, it was clearly not some epidemic as they all died at different times, and the most likely explanation is that it was a genetic disorder. There are of course many of

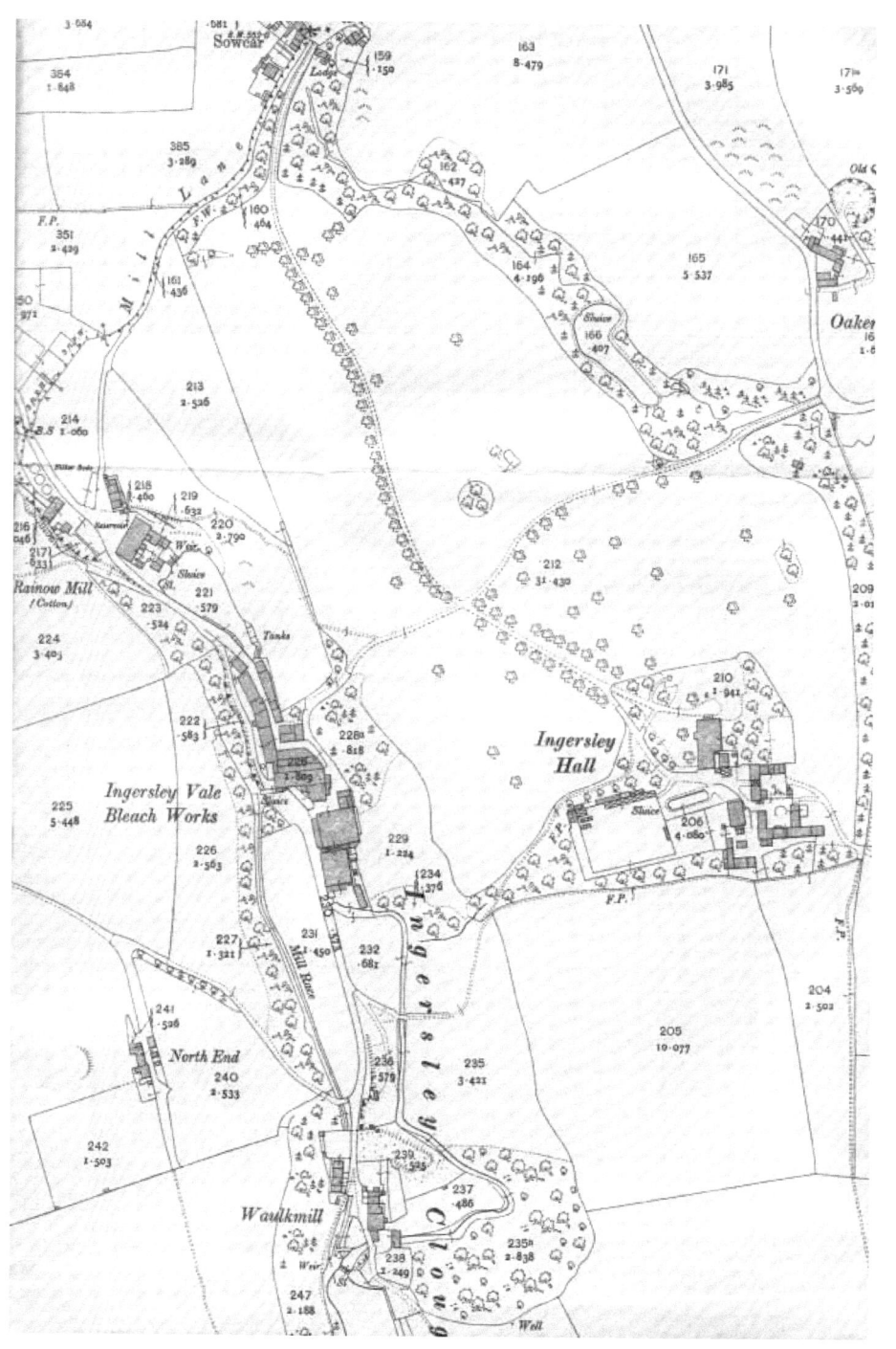

Map of 1907 showing Ingersley Hall and part of the estate, including Ingersley Farm adjacent to the Hall, the tree-lined drive running north west to the lodge, Rainow Mill, Ingersley Vale Mill and Waulkmill to the west, Oakenbank Farm to the north east, with nearby the start of the 'causeway' across the parkland to the Hall.

these, and they would have been less treatable and more likely to cause early death than today. Evidence from the next generation suggests it was some form of rheumatic disease, but whatever the cause it must have been a profound shock and something almost beyond endurance, to see so much hope and promise lost to grief and prolonged mourning over so many years.

Despite, or perhaps because of this, John of Ingersley set about not only developing and improving the estate at Ingersley, but acquiring new property. It is almost certainly he who enclosed the land on the Ingersley side of Kerridge Hill, formerly common land, with some of it used for farming purposes and some as shelter belts and plantations. Trees were planted in Ingersley Clough below the house, and managed for timber. This was a valuable commodity at the time and there is evidence of the Gaskells selling oak, ash, birch, elm, alder, thorn, crab and hazel in Bollington in 1824.[26] In addition gardens were created round Ingersley House with ornamental parkland beyond, the latter being a fashionable adjunct to grand country houses under the influence of the famous landscape gardener, Capability Brown.

Waulk Mill Farm in the wooded Ingersley Clough, first half of 20th Century.

John of Ingersley also probably rebuilt or improved the tenanted farms on the estate, including Ingersley Farm adjacent to Ingersley House, Higher Ingersley Farm, North End Farm, Waulk Mill Farm, Oakenbank Farm and Lima Farm. (At different times in this period another unrelated John Gaskell was tenant of the farms at North

End, Waulk Mill and Ingersley Hall, and later a James Gaskell at Ingersley Hall Farm.) John of Ingersley had of course also inherited the tenanted estates from his forebears, including Ollerenshaw and part of the land at Longdoles, as well as the more local properties at Tower Hill, Hedgerow and Orme's tenement, to which were added Sowcar after his brother Francis died in 1813, and at some stage premises in Disley and Kettleshulme. His main new acquisition was the estate of Hockerley, near Whaley Bridge, which included the early seventeenth century Hockerley Hall, still largely unaltered and another listed building. At first he had owned it jointly with Brocklehurst relatives, but by 1811 he had become the sole owner, keeping on as tenant farmers the Wild family who had been there over many generations.

As well as this impressive portfolio, John of Ingersley had an eye for property development. He acquired land on which to build dwellings both at Billinge (on Blaze Hill), and in several streets in Bollington. He was not alone in this, for Bollington was undergoing a period of rapid growth driven by the development of the cotton industry, and for the first time the population of Bollington was beginning to overtake that of Rainow. In the time John Gaskell was living at Ingersley, five or six mills were built in Bollington, which led to a need for workers and concomitantly, housing. Indeed, as well as housing, John of Ingersley had some involvement in the

Ingersley Vale Mill c1930

development of the mills themselves. In 1784 he was instrumental in building Mill Brook Mill in the centre of Rainow, probably on the site of a former corn mill. With the agreement of a local farmer he diverted Mill Brook to create a pond to provide a head of water to power the mill, used for cotton spinning. It was extended in 1805 and managed at different times by Samuel Joule and Sons, and Stephen and John Sheldon, who operated various mills in the area. After a fire in 1868 cotton spinning ceased and the partially rebuilt premises were used for fustian cutting.[27] The much larger Ingersley Vale Mill, first named Ingersley Clough Mill but also sometimes referred to as Ingersley Hall Mill, was built by John of Ingersley in 1792 or 1793 as a cotton spinning mill, although it was his son Thomas who had more of an interest in it (see below).

John of Ingersley also had the ownership, or possibly the lease, of one of the cotton mills in Bollington. The exact location of this latter mill is unknown but it was managed by the cotton spinner John Sheldon and referred to in John of Ingersley's will as 'Mrs Hill's cotton factory'. Another venture was to allow a mill reservoir to be built on land he held at the bottom of Ingersley Road to supply Oak Bank Mill. And like his father before him, John developed the coal potential on his holdings, both at Ingersley, with coal workings at North End and at Ingersley Vale, and at Hockerley, where the mines lay conveniently near the new canal, opened in 1800.

Whilst major industrial change was taking place at home, this was against the backdrop of the turbulence of the French wars. The French Revolution occurred in 1789, leading to the rise of Napoleon Bonaparte and his ambition to control Europe and defeat the British. There was a real fear in this country not only of a revolution inspired by the French, but also of invasion, with both possibilities particularly exercising the aristocracy and landed gentry who did not want to see their prosperity and way of life endangered. War between Britain and France broke out in 1793, and ebbed and flowed for a number of years, but France was eventually defeated in 1815 at the Battle of Waterloo. The significance of this victory was immense, and the Duke of Wellington, who had led the campaign, was given a hero's welcome on his return. There was celebration throughout the land, and a number of monuments and memorials were erected.

One of these monuments was built by John of Ingersley. As a member of the landed gentry, the assurance that after all life could continue as before must have been something of a relief, but he also had a personal link to the French wars. This was not in a fighting capacity, for the Gaskells had never been involved in the armed forces (and were not to be so for another three generations), but through family connections. His only surviving son Thomas was married to Mary Upton Slack, whose brother James, born in 1780, lived in Paris. James was detained as a prisoner of war at Valenciennes during the French wars, in effect interned. From a contemporary account it appears that 'Mr Slack', being a gentleman, was reasonably well-treated within the prison and able to socialise with those of similar status.

However he did not survive, dying in 1812 of a 'contagious disease' said to be caught from the far more harshly treated French deserter inmates.[28]

The monument that John of Ingersley built was at the northern end of the ridge of Kerridge Hill above Ingersley, on the boundary both of Gaskell land and of Rainow and Bollington. It took the form of a folly (an architectural device long in vogue with landowners) and was shaped like an old-fashioned conical sugar loaf (see cover illustration, taken about 1910). It was built of stone and had an iron studded wooden entrance door which opened into the small interior space. This contained a central circular stone table and stone benches set against the wall. In effect it functioned as a summer house, and no doubt the family used it both as a destination for picnics and as a point from which they could survey their land and property spread out below.

From the beginning the building was whitewashed, although given its exposed position the paint frequently flaked off and had to be replaced. During the two world wars it was camouflaged green, and in 1935, after the Gaskells had left Ingersley, it received a new coat of white-painted plaster in honour of the silver jubilee of King George V. Some years later the door was sealed up and plastered over to prevent vandalism.

The little monument became known as White Nancy, but there is some controversy as to when and how it was so styled. There are a number of well-rehearsed myths that suggest it was named either after the lead horse of the eight that pulled the stone up the hill, or after John of Ingersley's sister Nancy. However, it was not called White Nancy when first built, and was probably referred to simply as 'the summer house'; indeed Bryant's 1831 map of Cheshire shows it marked on a map as precisely that: 'summer house'. In fact in the early 1800s and probably before, the northern end of Kerridge Hill was called Northern Nancy, and there is evidence that this usage continued late into the nineteenth century and beyond, with the slopes of the hill being known as Nancy side.[29]

The word Nancy itself can be interpreted as deriving from 'ordnance', and reflects the fact that there had long been an ordnance beacon on the site in the shape of a rotunda of brick. Such beacons were maintained by the Board of Ordnance as part of the country's defence system, and 'ordnance points' stood in a chain across high ground ready to be lit at times of national emergency, or indeed of celebration. As it happens, the Duke of Wellington was appointed as Master General of the Ordnance in 1819, a few years after returning from his French victory.

A comment from John of Ingersley's great-granddaughter Anne Theodora suggested that the name White Nancy became attached to the hill before the monument, as she says in a letter of 1921: 'My great-grandfather caused the Sugar Loaf on White Nancy to be built in remembrance of the Battle of Waterloo'.[30] Certainly when I was a child growing up in Kerridge in the 1950s, that end of the hill was referred to as White Nancy, and the phrase 'going up White Nancy' meant taking a walk up the hill. Thus it would seem that (northern) Nancy was first a hill (named for a beacon), then the word 'white' was added to reflect the whiteness of the structure built upon it, and then in more recent times, after the departure of the Gaskells, the structure itself became 'White Nancy'.

The true sequence of events may be lost in the mists of time, but the former summer house has become an iconic landmark and a much loved local attraction. Indeed it has been adopted by the town of Bollington as its emblem, despite the fact that the boundary line, once a wall, then a fence, later a railing, and now a line of flagstones, indicates that by far the major part lies within Rainow. Now a Grade II listed structure, it remains today both a picnic destination and a place of celebration and commemoration, with the latter aspects being sometimes physically depicted on the body of White Nancy itself. Thus in recent years it has been decorated as a Christmas pudding and a Father Christmas, was emblazoned in 2014 with a poppy to commemorate the outbreak of World War One, and, perhaps more fittingly, on the bicentenary of the Battle of Waterloo in 2015 it displayed the silhouettes of nineteenth century soldiers.

White Nancy as embellished in 2015.

John of Ingersley died early in 1824 at the age of 80. He had undoubtedly been a man with impressive foresight and drive; creating a new family home, developing the land, and using that land to respond to the needs of the burgeoning industrial era in relation to coal mining, cotton spinning and housing. Both he and his wife, who had died six years earlier, are buried in the churchyard at Prestbury in the same tomb as their deceased children and John and Elizabeth of Sowcar.

In John of Ingersley's will he is styled as John Gaskell of Ingersley Esq., and his executors were his two nephews Richard Orford (the younger) and David Clayton. His main properties, including Ingersley, went to his only surviving child Thomas, whilst his many grandchildren also benefited both from monetary bequests and from land and property. He did not forget the poor of Rainow: 50 shillings were to be distributed in one shilling loaves on Love Sunday every year; and the school (i.e. the Sunday school, founded in 1820) was to have £1 yearly to cover the cost of teaching poor children. These amounts were to come from the interest on his investment in the new turnpike road from Macclesfield to Kerridge.

The will must have caused some problems as it was not proved until 5 May 1831, more than seven years after John of Ingersley's death. One complicating factor was the death of two of the grandchildren who had been given legacies, but probably more significant was the fact that Ingersley had been sold unlawfully by the Downes, as noted above. From the various deeds it would appear that Ingersley was conveyed back to copyhold status, and it was entered as such in the register of 1836 and even as late as 1885.[31]

4. A New Generation at Ingersley

John of Ingersley's son Thomas (1769-1830) succeeded to Ingersley after his father's death, moving there from Tower Hill where he had lived with his family. He was already 53 and enjoyed only six years at Ingersley before he died after a period of poor health. He also seems to have endured straitened circumstances in his later life. This was due perhaps in part to the fact that his father's will had still not been proved, which may have affected his access to income, and also to the fact that from 1826 there was a depression which caused a slump in trade and property prices.

Tower Hill House, early 20th century, then painted white, former home of the Brocklehursts, later the Gaskells. Rainow Church is centre left.

Thomas seems to have had some interest in the cotton trade and is listed in a directory of 1820 as cotton spinner at Tower Hill. It is therefore possible that he was involved in what became known as Cow Lane Mill but was originally known as Tower Hill Mill, located on the River Dean not far from Tower Hill. There is considerable uncertainty about the ongoing history of this mill, although it is believed it was built in 1789 as a cotton spinning mill and later converted to silk.[32] Thomas certainly had involvement with Ingersley Vale Mill, which, as noted above, was built on Gaskell land about 1792. It was managed by Edward Collier for a few years until he went bankrupt in 1811. Thomas had the mill rebuilt after a fire in 1819, and then went into partnership with Martin Swindells, although some accounts suggest he only leased it to Swindells. It was a substantial cotton spinning mill, and in 1826 had 330 looms operated by power from a water wheel, fed by a long leat from a large pool and dam situated near the old Waulk Mill. There was also a steam engine for when there was an insufficient head of water. In addition to the mill, there were some workers' cottages, an apprentice house for some 30 pauper apprentices, a shop, a smithy and a Sunday school. Although it is not clear precisely when these were built, they must have been approved and supported by the Gaskells, perhaps following the example of the Gregs at Quarry Bank Mill at Styal a few miles away. After Thomas' death his son John Upton acted as the proprietor, and in 1842 he had occasion to advertise it, listing the many benefits of the site.[33]

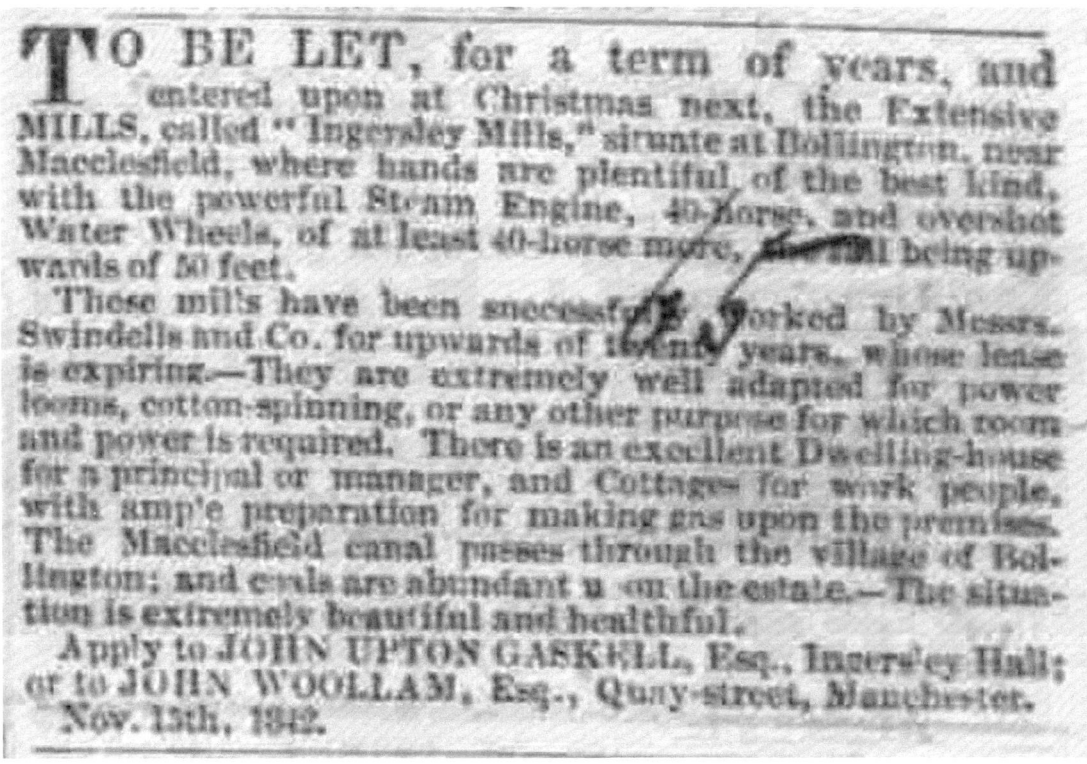

Advertisement for the letting of Ingersley Mill in The Manchester Courier and Lancashire General Advertiser *19 November 1842*

In 1801 Thomas Gaskell made what would have been considered a very good marriage, to Mary Upton Slack, with the ceremony being held at the prestigious Manchester Cathedral where Mary herself had been christened. The Slacks had been a landowning family in east Cheshire from at least the sixteenth century and were particularly associated with the Dunge in Kettleshulme, but also had other land in Cheshire and elsewhere. Mary's father was Abraham Slack, gentleman, of Longsight and Ardwick, a descendant of the Kettleshulme Slacks. Mary's mother, also Mary, had been the only surviving heir of John Upton of Chorlton, Manchester, and it is due to this connection that the Upton name has been passed down the Gaskell generations as a middle name to the present day.

Saltersford Church, endowed by the Slacks, and where the children of Thomas Gaskell were baptised

Thomas and Mary had 10 children; two sons and eight daughters, all born at Tower Hill. In a departure from the usual practice these children were baptised not as babies but in batches; the first eight on 6 January 1814, and the last two, Harriet and Richard, on 30 July 1827, all at the little church at Saltersford which had been endowed by John Slack of Kettleshulme, a relative of Thomas's wife Mary Upton Slack. Sadly, however, as in the previous generation several died young. The first born child Mary died in 1826 aged 23, the fourth child Ann died in 1820 aged 13, the fifth child Thomas in 1825 aged 16, whilst the ninth child Richard managed to outlive his father, dying in 1849 at the age of 32.

These deaths lend further support to the idea of a genetic disorder, and a possible clue comes from the death of Richard, the only one to occur after the new system of death certification was introduced in 1837. The cause was given as chronic rheumatism and acute pericarditis – the latter being caused by the former. Further support for the notion that the problem was rheumatic is provided by the fact that Richard's sister Mary was taken to Bath a few months before her death at the age of 23, almost certainly 'taking the waters'. It is possible therefore that all these young people suffered from a condition such as juvenile rheumatoid arthritis, which would have been far more crippling then than now.

Thomas Gaskell died in 1830 at the age of 61 and was buried in the churchyard at St Peter's, Prestbury in a tomb bearing the inscriptions of himself, his wife, his wife's brother John Slack, seven of his children, and his uncle, Francis of Sowcar. He had amassed considerable property by the time of his death, for in addition to his own inheritances he seems to have acquired premises on which he held mortgages, together with dwellings, factories and land both in Yorkshire and Lancashire. In his will he left his wife £5000 and Ingersley House with its land and all the household goods, carriages, horses, cattle etc. After her death these were to go to his eldest son, John Upton, who in the meantime was to have the two farms of Ingersley and Waulk Mill. The younger son Richard received the estate at Hockerley and the premises in Derbyshire (possibly Ollerenshaw or Nightwigg or both). The property that was mortgaged to Thomas was to go to his wife, and the property in Lancashire and Yorkshire was to be sold and the proceeds invested for his daughters. This was to be for their sole use and specifically not to pay the debts of any husband, 'neither shall such Husband or Husbands have any power or authority or control over the same'.

After her husband's death Mary lived on at Ingersley House with most of her children, the youngest, Richard, being only 14 at the time. A few months before Thomas' demise she had suffered another bereavement in that her older brother, John Slack, had died. It appears that he lived with them at Ingersley for some reason, perhaps due to illness. As a consequence of his death Mary acquired the property and land that had been passed down from her mother, and she also bought on her own account land in Newton, Lancashire.

Mary herself died in 1851 aged 77, two years after her son Richard. Her will is interesting in that it makes no mention whatsoever of her sole surviving son, John Upton. He had of course been provided for in his father's will in that he was to inherit Ingersley House and estate after his mother's death, but contrary to this will, Mary left all the household goods, carriages, horses, cattle etc. to her daughters. One of her daughters, Elizabeth, also received the Slack inheritance. Her father-in-law John

Gaskell had left various items of property to his young grandchildren but over the years Mary had purchased these from them, and now left them in trust to her daughters, in effect returning them whence they came. Most of her remaining property and money were to be invested to provide her daughters with an income. Her executors were her sons-in-law John Litton and Thomas Colville (notably not her son). The value of her estate was close to the not inconsiderable sum of £40,000, twice what her husband Thomas' had been.

Gaskell graves in the churchyard of St Peter's Prestbury.

The tomb of Thomas and his family is the taller one in the background. Thomas' parents John and Betty of Ingersley and four of their children, together with Thomas' grandparents John of Sowcar and his wife, are buried in the tomb in the foreground. The flat gravestone of Thomas' great grandparents John and Ellen is to the right of Thomas' tomb, and Thomas' great-great grandfather William of Adlington lies under the slightly raised stone, the edge of which can just be seen front right.

The children of Thomas and Mary who survived into adulthood were John Upton (1804-1883), Elizabeth (1806-1851), Frances (1810-1862), Ellen (1811-1895), Jane

(1813-1880), Harriet (c1815-1904) and Richard (1817-1849), although as we have seen the last named lived only until the age of 32. John Upton went on to inherit Ingersley and is discussed further below. Elizabeth married John Litton of Warrington, a corn merchant, who had inherited property from an uncle at Daresbury. Frances and Ellen never married. Harriet remained unmarried for many years, then at the age of 47 she became the wife of Thomas Michael Colville, a solicitor in Macclesfield.

Jane married the Reverend George Palmer, who had come to Bollington from Middlesex in 1839 as curate of the church of St John the Baptist. This had only been completed five years previously and was a chapelry under the main parish church at Prestbury. However, in 1842 Bollington became a separate parish and Geoffrey Palmer was appointed to be the first Vicar. He and Jane lived initially in Bollington Cross, then with their six children at the new vicarage (now demolished) adjacent to the church. Geoffrey suffered continual anxiety over church finances and it was this that probably exacerbated his ill health and hastened his premature death in 1852. He is buried in the churchyard at St John's, and the stained glass East window was created as a memorial to him. Jane remarried, and lived in Cheltenham with her new husband the Reverend Thomas Norwood, a fossil expert as well as a vicar. She died on a visit to Florence and is buried in the English cemetery outside the city (where some years ago I by chance saw her grave whilst looking for the memorial to a relative of my own).

Richard, the last of Thomas and Mary's children, proved to be the person who, despite his short life, illustrated how far the Gaskells had risen from the status of henchmen of the Leghs. This was through his marriage in 1841 to Mary Ann Turner. She was the daughter of William Turner of Flaxmoss House in Haslingden, Lancashire, a mill owner. William Turner's aunt, Jane Turner, had married her first cousin, another William Turner, a mill owner in Blackburn and an MP. In 1819 this latter William bought Shrigley Hall near Bollington from the virtually bankrupt Downes family. William and Jane's daughter Ellen became notorious for being abducted from boarding school at the age of 15 and forced into marriage at Gretna Green. The couple then escaped to France but were traced, returned, and the marriage annulled.[34] Two years later, in 1828, Ellen was married to Thomas Legh of Lyme Hall, himself illegitimate.

The fact that Richard Gaskell was able to meet Mary Anne Turner, Ellen's first cousin once removed, suggests that the Gaskells were socialising at Shrigley Hall, or at least in common company with the Turners, and, by association, with the Leghs. The marriage of Richard and Mary Anne also meant that the Gaskells and the Leghs became related by marriage. Unfortunately we will never know if there was a sense of satisfaction in this, and whether it was perceived as a significant step in their journey from hired hand to gentry.

Richard and Mary Anne lived at Tower Hill, where Richard died in 1849, having had no children. In his will, dated three years earlier, he bequeathed to his wife his carriages and horses and some household effects, but as she was well provided for by her father he left the rest of his to his sisters 'for their separate use and without the control or interference of any husband'. As noted above, his estate included the land and properties he had inherited from his father at Hockerley and in Derbyshire (perhaps Ollerenshaw or Nightwigg or both), and premises he had inherited at Bollington Cross from his grandfather. He instructed his executors, his brothers-in-law John Litton and Geoffrey Palmer (not his own brother), to manage the capital, interest and income of this property in trust for his sisters as they saw fit, and it may be at this time that both Ollerenshaw and Tower Hill were sold. Hockerley certainly stayed within the family, with Richard's sisters and some of their children continuing to own mining rights on the land farmed by the Wilds for many years.

5. The Life of a Country Squire

It was two decades after his father's death before John Upton finally inherited Ingersley. This had been left to his mother, whilst John Upton had the two tenanted farms at Ingersley and Waulk Mill. But he also possessed four freehold shops and offices in Cateaton Street and Victoria Street in central Manchester. One of the offices in Victoria Street bore the eponymous name Ingersley Chambers and was at the time occupied by S. Kershaw and Son, the Gaskells' land agents. These premises, and possibly others, may have been held back by John Upton rather than sold as directed in his father's will.

There was probably good reason as to why his father had seen fit not to bequeath him Ingersley when he was still such a young man. For John Upton had not proved able to live within his means, and seemed to think that as a gentleman he had a position to keep up in society, which entailed possessing, and even flaunting, the appropriate trappings. This sense of entitlement comes over in the 13 letters which survive from his time at Oxford University, spanning the years 1824-1830.[35]

Before becoming the first Gaskell to go up to Oxford, John Upton had been a pupil at Dr Davies' School in Macclesfield. This school had been founded in the sixteenth century as the Free Grammar school of Edward VI and at the time John Upton was a pupil it was located in King Edward Street. It had six classes, and was named Dr Davies' school after the headmaster, a Cambridge man, who was there from 1790-1828. It later became the King's School, still in existence in Macclesfield today as a fee-paying establishment. The intention was for John Upton to gain a degree in order to become a man of the cloth, one of the few suitable occupations for a gentleman's son, with the specific ambition that he eventually become Vicar of the new St John's Church in Bollington. It is not clear why this decision was made, but presumably at the time his father Thomas was expecting to live to the same advanced age as his own father, which would leave John Upton two decades of waiting to inherit Ingersley with no adequate income. Perhaps another element was a concern that he was profligate, and studying to be ordained would instil in him a sense of responsibility and humility.

At Oxford he attended Magdelen Hall, and studied several disciplines including divinity, ironically the subject with which he struggled most. He took a total of six years to gain his BA, then another year for his MA, failing and re-sitting various examinations, and complaining all the while about how hard he had to work. But his perception of his reason for being at Oxford was perhaps slightly different to that of his parents:

'As I did not come to Oxford for the express purpose of taking my degree only, but of introducing myself into respectable society, as well as seeing a little of the world, there was no occasion for me to work night and day for my degree as some do without any enjoyment whatsoever, [nor is there] a fat living waiting for me or some very great advantages depending upon it.'

What strikes one most about the letters he wrote is the number of times he asks for money. His first letter, dated 30th October 1824, shows how he is acquainting himself with the basic costs of tuition and lodging, plus the additional expenses of living in suitable style. One of his fellow students told him: 'a man could not live respectable as a gentleman under £300 a year'. Living as a gentleman required having a stock of good wine from London, possessing a smart horse and gig, riding to hounds with the Duke of Beaufort ('there's no sport like it'), and taking a continental tour. He is clearly conscious both of the constraints on 'my father's purse' and of his father's poor health (there is frequent reference to a bad and swollen leg), but this does not stop his constant demands for money, usually the sum of £100. Indeed he is criticised from home for his extravagance, with his sister Frances in particular berating him in an 'imperative manner'. He feels quite aggrieved about this:

I had intended to have said much about my horse and about getting a gig and harness for him, but since I have received my sister's letter I see that it is of no use and I will do my endeavour to dispose of my horse in the best manner I am able; I have got the saddler to take the harness back to my great grief, for it is such beautiful plain harness. With respect to my debts in Oxford, my dear Mother, you do not need to make yourself uncomfortable about them, because they are not so great but that I shall soon be able to pay them.'

It later transpires that he was unable to bring himself to part with either horse or gig, despite the fact that it seems to be his belief that no-one could be more 'frugal and economical'. In his opinion adequate funds were essential, for without them it: 'would have been impossible to keep respectable company [and] the company of my equals and those who are my brothers'. In another letter he somewhat imperiously demands that his father transfer to him the estate of Hockerley, and although this appears to be more to do with thereby qualifying for the shooting rights, it cannot have been lost on him that an income would also derive from it. (His father obviously did not agree, and in a form of comeuppance perhaps, later left Hockerley to his younger son Richard.)

John Upton's most expensive undertaking was probably his excursion to Europe; not quite the 'Grand Tour' as it was confined to the summer vacation of 1827. His trip, which he undertook with friends, was to take him to northern France, then to Belgium (at the time part of the Netherlands), where he planned to visit the 'celebrated Waterloo', then on to Germany, Switzerland and Italy, before returning via Paris. He was much affected in Brussels to be in the company of: 'some persons of great distinction, a <u>Russian Prince</u>, an <u>Italian Count</u>, and an <u>English Lord</u> [underlining in original]', the Italian Count being one of the people with whom he went to view 'the plains of Waterloo'. At the time, Waterloo was a famous battleground site, much as those of the Great War are today, but John Upton provides no indication as to what he made of it.

His mother had wanted him to visit Valenciennes to see if he could find the burial place of her brother James, who, as noted above, had died in prison during the French wars. However, John Upton considered it was too far out of his way:

> You spoke of Valenciennes and the probability of my uncle's being buried there: we are at least 70 miles distant from it, and do not expect to be any thing [*sic*] nearer in the course of our tour: would it not therefore be inexpedient to pop over there 70 miles and the same number back again in all 140 miles without the certainty of finding that my uncle was buried there. Did we know for certainty that the ashes were there deposited and if any good could result from visiting the place, we would certainly do so, but this is not the case and therefore we think it prudent to decline.'

In Paris, where he was: 'almost bewildered by the gay and glittering objects everywhere presented to view', he did try making enquiries about his uncle, but whilst he tracked down someone who had known him, he could not discover anything further about his affairs.

John Upton had no sooner been awarded his first degree at Oxford than his father died. It seems there was then no question of him becoming a vicar, but one can only imagine that it was a huge disappointment to him not to inherit Ingersley immediately, and to see his younger brother, still aged only 14, receiving Hockerley. After completing the additional term at Oxford necessary to receive his MA he went home to live at Ingersley House with his mother and younger sisters. But even if he did not then own Ingersley House, it is apparently due to his influence that at this time it was extended and renamed Ingersley Hall.

The extensions occurred in two phases, the first in 1833 and the second later, possibly not until after his mother's death. The earlier extension was on the north side and involved creating a grand new main entrance, built in the fashionable Greek revival style and complete with Doric porch (as illustrated on the back cover). The second extension was a larger wing to the south side, and the new south door was fitted with the Tuscan doorcase of the old main entrance from the west front. When completed the Hall had a total of 28 rooms, including a ballroom, with cellars below.

As well as considering how to improve his home John Upton also turned his attention to local affairs. He continued his father's interest in the establishment of a church in Bollington, and in 1834 he presented the letter of consecration of the newly founded St John's Church to the Bishop. A few years later he was one of the six committee members on the board which established, financed and oversaw the church school. He would also have been involved in the local celebrations for the 1837 coronation of Queen Victoria when his mother hosted entertainment for the schoolchildren at Ingersley Hall. He took on more formal appointments too: in 1836 at the age of 32 he was made a magistrate, a role that lasted throughout his life; and in the same year he was appointed a land tax commissioner for Cheshire. This period would therefore seem to mark the transition from being a rather self-absorbed young man to becoming one with a sense of responsibility and commitment, and with duties to perform.

Ingersley Hall with original house on the right, new wing and main entrance on the left. The identity of the people is unknown but probably includes members of the Gaskell family.

A few years later a further step in this direction was marked when at the relatively late age of 39 he entered into marriage. The ceremony took place at Taxal Church on 13th December 1843 and, perhaps appropriately, was officiated by the then head of the Grammar School John Upton had attended, the Reverend Osborne. His bride was Margaret Elizabeth Grimshawe (1813-1887), daughter of Samuel Grimshawe (1768-1851) who had recently built Errwood Hall in the Goyt Valley near Taxal.[36] Samuel Grimshawe was a wealthy merchant in Manchester, and like John Upton's great-uncle Thomas, a member of the Shaw Club. He had built Errwood Hall as a country residence for the family, but they also had a house in Manchester and one in London. Samuel's son, also Samuel (1808-1883), was at Brasenose College at Oxford at a time that overlapped with John Upton. The Gaskells and Grimshawes therefore probably knew each other socially even before the move to Errwood, whilst thereafter it was only a short ride over the moors to participate in hunting parties and other social events. Also, either before or after his marriage, John Upton and the younger Samuel Grimshawe had coalmining interests in common: not only did they both have mines on their land but they also had a mine near Paris to which they regularly travelled.

Errwood Hall in the Goyt Valley, c1900, home of the Grimshawes

After the marriage John Upton and Margaret settled not at Ingersley but at Endon House in Kerridge. This, along with the nearby and much grander Endon Hall, had been built in the 1830s by his father's cousin, William Clayton, after he had bought Endon Quarry. Presumably John Upton and his new wife did not want to start their married life sharing a house with John Upton's mother, and Endon House was a not dissimilar size to the original Ingersley House, with pleasant gardens but no significant land. It was accessed by a driveway from what is now Windmill Lane above Kerridge, and the solid stone gateposts engraved 'Endon House' still stand at the entrance. Their first child Anne Theodora was born at Endon House on 6th October 1844, and the birth was announced in a number of newspapers, including the London *Morning Post*. This stated in the birth column on 16th October: 'at Endon House, near Macclesfield, [to] the lady of John Upton Gaskell Esq, a daughter'.

In 1850 John Upton and his family moved back to Ingersley Hall, presumably because his mother, Mary Gaskell, by then 76, was in need of assistance. It would appear from the census of 1851 however, that they still had two separate households: Mary had 40 acres and resided with two of her adult daughters, together with three servants, a coachman and a gardener all living in; whilst John Upton had 27 acres, and lived with his wife and daughter, a governess named Henrietta Henread, from Normandy, and seven outdoor labourers.

On 1st June 1851 Mary Gaskell's life came to an end, thus finally allowing John Upton to become the owner of Ingersley. Earlier in that same year his wife Margaret's father, Samuel Grimshawe, had also died, and she inherited his house, offices and premises at 48 King Street in Manchester. Samuel was interred at Manchester Cathedral, but his wife Anne, who had died a few months earlier, was buried at Taxal Church. Here a plaque in memory of them both was erected by Margaret and John Upton. In the following year, on 26th March 1852, their son and heir John Francis Upton was born, the birth being again widely announced in local and national newspapers.

About this time further costly works were carried out at Ingersley. These included the addition of conservatories to the side of the south front, the extension of the farmhouse (now listed) to provide more accommodation and a small barn with cart entrance at the rear, and extravagant new stable blocks and coach houses which, as indicated by datestones, were built in 1853, 1856, 1858 and 1859. These were home to John Upton's many horse and carriages, for throughout his life he was a lover and breeder of horses, as well as a sportsman and a follower of the Cheshire Hunt.

The conservatory and coach house at Ingersley Hall, about 1900. The south door is just visible on the left. The identity of the gentleman is unknown.

The grounds and parkland also received his attention, with improvements to the gardens, including the walled kitchen garden, and the placing of a haha near the north front, and it may well be he who at this time created a lake by the damming of the stream that ran under what is now referred to as 'the causeway'. Probably also he was responsible for further tree planting, as well as the enclosure of more land and the consolidation of boundaries. In this regard there exists a boundary stone (now listed) set into the wall where a shelter belt meets the boundary at the top of Kerridge Hill. On the western side, as illustrated below, the stone bears the initials T G and the date 1839; G standing for Gaskell and T being the owner, possibly Turner, of the land on that side of the boundary. On the eastern, Ingersley side, the date is lacking and the characters are more simply carved.

Boundary stone in the wall at the top of Kerridge Hill

There is no evidence John Upton had any involvement with Ingersley Vale Mill, other than owning the land on which it stood, and indeed he specifically said in the hearing referred to below that he was not a 'factory' owner. However, he did manage Ingersley Farm himself, raising horned dairy cattle and small numbers of limestone sheep (a now extinct Peak District breed), and growing hay and root crops. Only when he reached the age of 70 did he feel the need to give this up, with the livestock and farm equipment all going to auction. Included were a total of 24 cows and calves with a bull; five well bred horses, one being a chestnut gelding 'broken to harness, and has carried a lady'; two pigs; numerous poultry; a few tons of 'mangold wurtzels' and even a canoe. The farmhouse, previously occupied by the gardener, was advertised to let along with 85 acres.[37]

*Ingersley Hall Farm about 1900.
The figures are probably the Coopers, tenants at the time.*

Some information about Ingersley and the life of its inhabitants at this time can be gleaned from a little children's book written by Margaret Gaskell in 1881, entitled *History of Good Dog Fanny and Tuft the Canary, With Other Stories All True*. Whilst there is probably an element of poetic licence, there is reference to various rooms within the house and some elements of the grounds: the library, with a bay window overlooking the garden; the dining room; the kitchen; the hall with a gas lamp set on a large bronze figure; the game larder, a stone building with a flagged floor at the back of the house; the saddle room and stables; 'the park'; the kitchen garden with its eight foot walls covered with fruit trees, and door locked at night. Not a great deal is written about the children, always known in the family as Annie and Francis, other than that Francis even at a young age liked to go out shooting with his dog Fanny, and that they had various pets, including three canaries and a dormouse. The latter kept Margaret herself amused when she was unwell for a long period and had to stay in bed unable even to read. When the dog Fanny got very old, a friend in London sent a new dog whose credentials were impeccably aristocratic:

> . . . a very pretty fox-terrier of quite a grand family. His papa belonged to a duke, and his mamma to an earl; and we were told, also, that his sister had been given to the Prince of Wales, and positively lived at his royal highness's house at Sandringham.

There is also mention of various servants in the book: a coachman, who exercised the horses every morning; Mary the maid; Willie the garden boy; and Martha and Ann, both cooks at different times. Particularly interesting is an account of the engagement of a French children's maid whose duties were to dress and play with the children and help them easily to pick up French by chatting to them. The selection was done on a visit to Paris where Margaret was advised to seek such a maid from the Protestant orphanage. The young girl she chose was one of two sisters, probably themselves barely in their teens:

> Madame called a bright-eyed, healthy looking girl from amongst the crowd. 'This', said she, 'is the little Elise; I think she will suit you. She is a good child, speaks the truth, and is clever with her needle'. I, of course, began to question Elise, and asked her if she would like to go to England and be a little nurse-maid. 'Oh yes; very much,' was the reply; and soon was all arranged with Madame H as to wages and clothes for the little girl.

The sisters had a grandmother who took an interest in their welfare, and at first she was (not surprisingly) opposed to one of her granddaughters going away to a foreign land where she might be ill-treated. However, when she was taken to see the flaxen haired and cherubic four year old Francis asleep in bed she was so moved by the sight of him that she called him 'a little angel' and gave her blessing to the arrangement.

Another servant referred to is Betty, who had been once been nurse to the Gaskells. She and her husband Laban, who had been a soldier, came to live rent free at the lodge at the gateway to Ingersley. This building (now demolished) is described as being surrounded by tall trees and having ivy covered walls, whilst within was one main room with an oven, one bedroom, and a little scullery. Betty washed and starched 'the squire's' shirts and all the children's clothes, and after Laban died she lived there alone. Annie and Francis used to enjoy visiting her with their maid and seeing her little canary Dicky, and to Margaret's obvious pleasure Betty 'was proud of my fat rosy boy.' When Betty died John Upton followed her coffin to the grave as a mark of respect to his mother's old servant.

The book also provides insight into the frequent holidays and excursions the family undertook, both at home and abroad. Information on some of the visits within this country can be also be gleaned from the social columns of newspapers, in which it was commonplace to list important visitors and the addresses where they were staying. Thus we can see, for example, that Mr and Mrs Gaskell of Ingersley were in

Leamington Spa in April and May 1850, in Brighton in February 1860, and in Whitby with their daughter in July and September 1871. There were also various trips to London, although there is no evidence the Gaskells had their own property there. It is possible they stayed with Margaret's Grimshawe family who are known to have had a London home.

Ingersley Hall Lodge, now demolished, c1920, with the then resident, Mrs Berry.

Paris was another city that was visited, not just on the occasion of the appointment of the French children's maid, but with frequent trips often for weeks at a time. This was no doubt due to the fact that it was in the vicinity of Paris that John Upton and his brother-in-law had some coal mining interests, although the precise nature of these is not clear. In her book, Margaret writes of the children enjoying the entertainments to be found in the Champs Elysées, and of how they were all thrilled by the lavish procession for the christening of the baby son of the Emperor Napoleon III and his wife.

The Grimshawes were also instrumental in facilitating vacations abroad, for Margaret's brother possessed a yacht called the *Mariquita* and the two families often voyaged together: John Upton, Margaret and their two children; and Samuel Grimshawe, his wife Jessie and their two daughters, Mary and Genevieve. There were yachting trips to Scotland (where they saw the Giant's Causeway), the Bay of Biscay, Gibraltar, and Italy, where they visited Naples:

It is indeed, a charming place from a distance, but when you enter it many of the streets are dirty and smell most unpleasantly; and it is sad to see the swarms of wretched women and children, and men too, lounging about in a state of misery and idleness. . . . They lie warming themselves in the sun more like animals than human beings. They eat black bread and miserable, hard-dried little figs . . .

On the same trip they made an excursion to Pompei, at the time still being excavated. Here they tried to buy a white marble statue of Venus, the size of a doll, with a gold necklace and bracelet, but were not allowed to do so as all finds were to go to a museum. However, both the Gaskells and the Grimshawes undoubtedly made many purchases of curiosities and keepsakes during these trips as both families were, like most landed gentry of the time, collectors of furniture, china, statues and paintings.

Amongst the paintings that John Upton acquired in this country were some with an interesting history as they had once belonged to Maria Letizia Bonaparte, the mother of Louis Napoleon. These had been bought from her in Rome by the 16th Earl of Shrewsbury, and following the death of the 17th Earl in 1857 they were sold at an auction at Alton Towers. One of the paintings John Upton bought (for £8.18sh.6d) was at the time thought to be by the artist Spagnoletto and to represent Archimedes, but was identified nearly 150 years later and long after it had passed out of Gaskell hands as a portrait of the Philosopher Tales by an Old Master, Jusepe de Ribera, thus significantly increasing its value.[38] Ironically, given the origin of the paintings, one of the other artefacts the Gaskells had collected was a marble statue of Marie Antoinette who was guillotined during the French revolution. The statue had lain buried in the Tuileries Gardens where Louis XVI and Marie Antoinette had been imprisoned and was probably purchased by the Gaskells in Paris.

As well as their travels, the Gaskells would have been in demand socially nearer home, for by now they were well-connected and their circle would have included all the local gentry. Thus John Upton Gaskell was one of those invited to Eaton Hall, south of Chester, when the Marquis of Westminster took up residence there. The Marquis, whose family had immense fortunes and owned large parts of London, had instigated an extensive programme of refurbishment. On completion of the project in September 1855 he invited the great and good of the county to celebrate his achievements. Amongst the guests were the Leghs of Lyme Park, the Brocklehursts of Macclesfield, and the Gregs of Quarry Bank Mill.[39] The fact that the Leghs of Lyme and the Gaskells were rubbing shoulders in this way serves to re-emphasise how far up the social ladder the Gaskells had climbed in five generations. Indeed this was further endorsed when in 1870 John Upton's daughter Anne Theodora was one of the seven bridesmaids for Florence Legh, daughter of Charles Legh of Adlington, distant cousins of the Leghs of Lyme. To be chosen as bridesmaid Anne Theodora must have been considered a social equal as well as a friend, and her parents were of course amongst the many guests.[40]

Given his position, it was inevitable that John Upton would be drawn into local affairs, but the evidence would seem to indicate that as he got older this was not just as a figurehead but with a sense of commitment and a desire to improve the lot of those around him. We have already seen that at a relatively young age he became involved in founding the church and the church school for Bollington, and this interest was extended to Rainow where he helped to secure the building of a church in 1845 and, many years later, gave sufficient funding to enable the ending of pew rents as a means to support the vicar's stipend. He also became treasurer of the Rainow Church and King Friendly Society and was enthusiastic in promoting its aims of assisting the poor.

In 1859 his responsibilities as a JP were increased when he was elected Chairman of the Bench for the Prestbury Division, a position he held until his death, as too was that of Chairman of the Conservative District (which included Bollington). Other causes concerned local infrastructure, particularly in relation to transport and the provision of services. There had been a suggestion by one of the mill owners that Bollington needed a railway line to connect it with Manchester and thus benefit both the cotton and the quarrying industries. The Macclesfield, Bollington and Marple Railway Bill was read and passed in Parliament in 1864, and John Upton became Chairman of the Company until it was taken into new ownership. He might have felt a personal interest in the proposed line as it cut through the Gaskell land at Longdoles in Adlington, although this had probably passed out of the family at this stage.

As well as this connection with the railway, John Upton was involved in matters to do with housing and working conditions in Bollington. Thus in 1861 he gave a witness statement in relation to the Macclesfield Gas Bill, and in 1862 made a further witness statement for the Bollington Improvement and Lighting Bill, passed into statute in the same year. In regard to the latter he was given quite a grilling at the hearing, as he had been chairman of the meetings of Bollington ratepayers at which improvements had been debated, as well as a key figure in promoting the Bill to Parliament. Interestingly, in the initial declarations he answered in the affirmative to the question as to whether he was a resident of the township of Bollington – strictly speaking he lived in Rainow.[41] When the latter Act was passed it allowed funds to be raised from ratepayers to improve public services such as drainage, lighting and highways for those parts of Bollington where the population had grown most rapidly following the expansion of the cotton mills. Improvements were certainly needed, especially in regard to sanitation and surface water. Flooding of the many cellars was frequent, with stagnant and contaminated water causing frequent disease and notably a severe outbreak of cholera in 1861.

In his late 70s John Upton's own health began to fail, and he died on 8th August 1883. He was buried in Prestbury churchyard in a polished granite tomb, a few yards from his ancestors. The inscription states:

In memory of John Upton Gaskell of Ingersley 47 years Magistrate for this County Died August 8th 1883 Interred August 11th his 79th Birthday. The upright shall dwell in thy presence Psalm 140 verse 13.

His rather fulsome obituary appeared in the local paper, beside a photograph of Ingersley Hall taken before the addition of the wing on the south side.[42]

John Upton's wife Margaret survived only another three and a half years, but she clearly continued to take an interest in local and national affairs. One issue which seems to have exercised her was that of a suitable monument to General Gordon, who was killed in 1885. Gordon had been something of a hero to the British public for his military campaigns overseas, not unlike the Duke of Wellington, and after his death there was much discussion about suitable memorials. There was a strength of feeling that something should be done to commemorate his work with poor and destitute boys, and that this was more appropriate than grand monuments. Responding to this debate, Margaret Gaskell wrote to a Manchester newspaper as follows:

> MEMORIAL TO GENERAL GORDON.
> *To the Editor of the Manchester Courier.*
> Sir,—If the suggestion from "An Englishwoman" is adopted as a memorial to General Gordon, instead of a senseless and most probably inartistic statue, by the inhabitants of Manchester, I feel certain that many Englishwomen in that city and its neighbourhood, would gladly assist in so good a cause; and if you would open a subscription list in your columns it would be quickly filled. You can insert Mrs. Gaskell, Ingersley, £10; Miss Gaskell, £5, amongst other names if "An Englishwoman's" proposal is adopted.—Yours, &c.,
> MARGARET ELIZABETH GASKELL.
> Ingersley Hall, near Macclesfield, March 31st.
> P. S.—As Gordon sent his gold medal to the Manchester Cotton Relief Fund the inhabitants of the city ought certainly to erect a memorial, which like this would have met with his full approbation.

Letter to Manchester Courier and Lancashire General Advertiser 1 April 1885

This letter was just one example of Margaret's commitment to philanthropic causes, for there were many she supported or for which she was a patroness. A similar disposition was instilled in her daughter, Anne Theodora, who as we shall see in the following chapter, was at least as benevolently inclined as her mother.

When John Upton died he left Ingersley Hall to his wife, and after her death to his daughter. His wife also received all his horses, carriages, wines and liqueurs (almost suggesting the latter two were as valuable as the former two), and the shops and offices in Manchester at Cateaton Street and Victoria Street. Ingersley Farm, Lima Farm, Oakenbank Farm, five cottages and a quarry also at Oakenbank, and 12 cottages and some land in Ingersley Road were similarly to go first to his wife, then his daughter. He had also amassed a considerable portfolio of additional property in Manchester, all of which was to left to his daughter. This included a number of freehold shops, offices and other premises in Ancoats, together with various chief rents, and a public house called the Blue Bell near the city centre. The rest of his estate was to go to his son John Francis. Although not specified this would presumably have included the farms at Higher Ingersley, Waulk Mill and North End, Ingersley Vale Mill, and the properties at Sowcar, Spuley, Hedgerow and Billinge, all of which had been in the Gaskell family for some time. It may also by this time have included Rainow Mill, a cotton mill and former corn mill situated near Ingersley Vale Mill, as this mill was certainly in the possession of John Upton's son a few years later.

The interesting detail that emerges from the proving of the will is that the gross amount of his estate was just £4513.1sh. 7d, a tenth of what his mother's had been. The implication is that all the improvements, acquisitions and pleasures of a somewhat lavish lifestyle had led to a degree of indebtedness; a situation perhaps predictable from those early days of aspirational and hedonistic extravagance.

6. The Last Gaskell at Ingersley

John Upton's daughter Anne Theodora (1844-1923) was nearly 40 when she inherited Ingersley after her father died. Her brother John Francis Upton (1852-1929) was some eight years younger, and had been expensively educated at Eton and Sandhurst, with a spell in the infantry regiment of the Royal Cheshire Militia. By this time he had lost the plumpness, rosy cheeks, and fair hair that his mother had so admired, and had become tall, dark and somewhat languid, as illustrated in the accompanying photograph. This also reveals that he had continued his childhood interest in shooting, as it depicts one of the many hunting parties in which he participated with his Grimshawe relations.

John Francis Gaskell, standing against right hand side of window, at a hunting party of the Grimshawes in 1881.

At Sandhurst he was a gentleman cadet, training to achieve a direct commission, and although he passed, his marks were somewhere near the bottom.[43] He joined the 6th Dragoon Guards as a sub-lieutenant and later lieutenant, eventually becoming a Captain with the Royal Scots Greys before resigning his commission in 1881. Both of these regiments consisted of mounted cavalry and he was thus enabled to continue professionally the association with horses (and guns) that had been so much a part of his early life. He was married in 1877 to Juliana Reed, daughter of Major Joseph Haythorne Reed, but as her parents had both died young she had been brought up by her Reed grandparents.

As a result of this marriage John Francis acquired East Brent Manor in Somerset, but much of his early married life was spent living in different parts of the country with his regiment. After he left the army he was able to live on his own means, and seems to have divided his time between Somerset and a house in Marylebone in London. The benefits of his career and his marriage meant that by the time his father died he was both well provided for and not in particular need of a residence. The unmarried Anne Theodora, however, was reliant on her father, and it is presumably for this reason that Ingersley was bequeathed to her.

Ingersley Hall in the time of Anne Theodora Gaskell, shown in its completed form with the addition of the three bay extension on the right.

As a girl and young woman Anne Theodora would have participated in the high society social events enjoyed by her parents, and accompanied them on trips to the fashionable resorts in this country and the more exotic locations abroad. The latter, as we have seen, were often in the company of her Grimshawe relations, and throughout her life she continued to be associated with them and to attend family events and social functions. Thus, for example, in 1883 she was one of the mourners at the burial of her uncle Samuel Grimshawe, a Catholic, at the private cemetery in the grounds of Errwood; in 1892 she attended the wedding of her cousin Genevieve in London, presenting her with a diamond pendant; and in 1895 she was one of the guests at a party given by the Grimshawes at Errwood Hall for their tenants and tradesmen. Both her cousins, Mary and Genevieve, outlived Anne Theodora and they too were buried in the private cemetery at their home. On at least one of those occasions Anne Theodora's nephew, the second John Upton Gaskell and his wife were present. Mary and Genevieve, having both married later in life, were childless, and hence the last in the line of Grimshawes at Errwood. Not long after their death Errwood Hall itself was demolished as part of the construction works for a new reservoir, leaving only some ruins to act as a focus of interest for visitors to the Goyt Valley.

By the time Anne Theodora inherited Ingersley her chances of marriage would have receded, even supposing that is what she wished for herself. As an unmarried older woman she would not have been in demand socially and was perhaps even looked upon with disdain in some quarters. She seems to have led a quiet and unpretentious life, devoting herself to her estate on the one hand, and becoming involved in 'good works' on the other. Indeed her dedication to philanthropic causes, in part instilled by her mother, could be seen as the culmination of a disposition which had been passed down through many generations of Gaskells from her forebears in Handley.

She supported charitable enterprises both locally and nationally, and also treated her servants and tenants well, providing them with occasional dinners at the Turners Arms in Bollington at her own expense. Problems of local hardship were a particular concern:

> Last week Miss Gaskell again showed her benevolence for the poor and needy of Rainow by giving presents consisting of bed quilts, blankets, coal, tea and coffee, and numerous other articles.[44]

She had a special interest in activities and institutions in her own parish of Rainow. For example she was President of the Horticultural Society and pledged significant amounts to support the annual Rainow Show, together with prizes of one guinea for the best cheese and butter. In February 1894, she gave an address at the welcome tea for the new Vicar, the Reverend W. Thomas, when 500 people sat down to tea in the church schoolroom. On the same occasion some 80 loaves were handed out to the poor of the parish – it must have been gratifying for Anne Theodora to know that the wishes of her great-grandfather, who had left money for this purpose, were still being carried out.

The Church and the school were also important to her: in 1878 she set the pendulum of the new church clock going; in 1896 she hosted at Ingersley the first annual sports day of the Church and King Friendly Society that her father had championed, providing handsome prizes; she bought Pedley Fold Farm so that the church could have extra ground for its graveyard; and she donated the land now known as Trinity Gardens as a playground for the school children so they could benefit from the fresh air and exercise she felt they needed.[45] This interest in children extended to the boys attending the Industrial School in Macclesfield. This had been founded in 1858 as the Ragged and Industrial School and eventually housed some 150 boys with a remit to train them for a trade. It was closed in 1922, the year before Anne Theodora died, and so did not benefit from the provision made in her will for recreational purposes.

At home Anne Theodora had two female companions, Mary Alice Catterall and Ethel Surplice, both of whom probably came to her soon after the death of her mother in 1887 and were certainly there in 1891. Ethel was presumably of military parentage as she was born in Rangoon in Burma, and both were a number of years younger than Anne Theodora. Over the years she also increased the number of servants living in the household. In 1881 her parents had managed with a cook and two other female servants living in, but Anne Theodora in 1891 had one man servant and four female servants, including a cook and a French maid. In both 1901 and 1911 there was the same male servant and five female servants: a cook; a head housemaid; two further housemaids; and a kitchen maid. With one exception all these resident servants were from outside the local area, and it is quite likely there were also one or two 'dailys' to do some of the menial tasks. There were in addition a number of outdoor staff, including a gardener, a coachman, two grooms, and a number of under gardeners, carters, and labourers, some of whom were housed in the cottages at Oakenbank.

Anne Theodora was severely ill towards the end of her life and spent the last three years confined to her room. Here she was tended by her faithful companions and a nurse, and regularly visited by her doctor, Dr John Hughes of Macclesfield. She died at home on 10th April 1923. Prior to her death she had requested that there was to be no fuss or ceremony, with no memorial service and no period of mourning. The only notice appeared in the newspaper four days later, on the day of the funeral itself: 'Friends kindly accept this the only intimation. No flowers by request.'[46] Later that same day she was buried with her parents in the churchyard at Prestbury. A short obituary in the same edition praised her philanthropic work:

> Miss Gaskell, years ago, took an active interest in many charitable organisations in and around Macclesfield. Of a very generous disposition, her name figured on the subscription list of every worthy object. A good cause always appealed to her and Bollington and Rainow particularly have good reason to be grateful to her for her unsparing devotion to the many good causes with which she associated herself.

At her death Anne Theodora's estate was worth the significant sum of nearly £107,400 (approximately £5,000,000 today) but was subject to the punitive death duties which had recently been increased. Her will continued in the same spirit of generosity that had marked her life, and many charities both near and far received substantial legacies. Locally these included £400 to be invested to increase the Vicar's stipend, and £850 to be invested and managed by the Vicar and wardens of Rainow Church. The income was to be used towards the running costs of the Church, Sunday School and National School, the purchase of clothes and coal for 'poor and deserving' parishioners, school prizes and an annual treat for the schoolchildren, and the 'purchase of buns to be distributed on Christmas Day among the scholars'.

She did not forget any of her servants, the most senior of whom were given quite large amounts, such as £300 to her gardener and her coachman. But all had at least a small sum, together with one quarter's wages and their mourning clothes. Even her land agent, George Kershaw in Manchester, was remembered: 'Fifty pounds to purchase a little remembrance of me and as a token of thanks for the care he has taken of my property'. Her two companions received annuities of £1000 each and various pieces of jewellery, whilst one of them, Mary Catterrall, was to have her choice of the wines and liqueurs, horses, ponies, dogs, carriages, saddlery and animal fodder. Mary was also charged with the task of examining all letters, documents and manuscripts, and destroying any which she deemed unnecessary to retain (thus accounting in part for why so little remains to illuminate the lives of the Gaskells).

Naturally, the bulk of Anne Theodora's effects went to her family, with various sums of money and annuities specified, and particular bequests relating to pieces of furniture and other items. These were obviously carefully selected according to the preferences or interests of each individual. Thus amongst other items her brother was to receive a gold snuff box, a Worcester tea set, a tortoiseshell and ivory cabinet bought in Granada, an ivory inlaid settle from the billiard room, and a cupboard and its contents from the gun room. Her brother's older daughter, Margaret Violet, was bequeathed an ebonized and gold cabinet and some Japanese china from the Red Room, and the younger daughter, Maud Ethel, a black oak cabinet and some Dresden, Worcester and Sèvres china. These were all to be kept as heirlooms and not to be sold. Even her young great nephews were remembered, with a coin and stamp collection for one, and a cello and piano for the other.

Ingersley and all her other property in Rainow and Bollington were left to her brother, and after his death to his older daughter, then to his younger daughter and her family. Her other personal assets and remaining property (unfortunately not specified) were left in trust to pay her legacies and bequests. Some of the property could be sold if necessary, but preferably not the land and buildings at 48 King Street, Manchester, which had belonged to her grandfather, Samuel Grimshawe, and had come to her through her mother. It is worthy of note that Anne Theodora specifically requested that the Cheshire property (which included Ingersley) was not to be disposed of but was to remain in the family.

7. After the Gaskells

After the death of Anne Theodora no other member of the Gaskell family lived permanently at Ingersley. However there were visits of varying durations over the next few years from the family of her brother John Francis, who now inherited the Ingersley estate. John Francis had three children by his wife Juliana: Margaret Violet (1880-1921); Maud Ethel (1884-1965); and John Upton (1886-1967). Juliana died in 1915 and some years later, in 1927 and only two years before he died, John Francis married Louise Sidley. She had been the children's governess when they were young and their friend as they grew older. The two girls married two brothers from a long-established family from Shawdon Hall in Northumberland; William Hargrave Trotter Pawson and Carnegie Robert Pawson, both of whom were in the army. Margaret Violet had only one child, William John, born in 1902, whilst Maud Ethel had two sons, Reginald Francis born in 1910, and Algernon John born in 1916. The sisters both later divorced and remarried, Margaret Violet to Henry Talbot Watson in 1911, and Maud Ethel to John Kennedy, a military man, in 1919. Margaret Violet died in 1921, two years before her aunt, Anne Theodora, and therefore when John Francis died in 1929, it was Maud Ethel who inherited Ingersley.

John Francis' youngest child, John Upton, had attended public school at Harrow and then entered the army, eventually fighting in the First World War as a lieutenant in the Royal Field Artillery. In 1912 he married Ethel Beatrice Hall (née Lloyd), a woman more than ten years older than himself, who was not only a divorcée but also an actress and renowned for her beauty. Possibly to the relief of the wider Gaskell family, John Upton followed the pattern of his sisters in being divorced and remarried, his second wife being Ursula Louise Dunsterville who came from the more acceptable background of a military family. His son by his first wife was Peter Upton (1913-1998), and he also had a son by his second wife, Richard Upton (1926-2003). Richard was the only one of this generation to be born at Ingersley, suggesting that his father still liked to reside there from time to time as well as at his home in the south. Indeed it would seem John Upton continued to have an interest in his grandmother's Grimshawe family too, as in 1930 he bought an expensive Spanish painting at the auction of the contents of her old home at Errwood Hall.

This interest in the family heritage did not endure however, as to the regret of later generations he subsequently disposed of much of the remaining family documents and other memorabilia. But there was one important aspect of his inheritance that he did retain, and which, moreover, was passed on to subsequent generations: the dedication to horses that had been so integral to his grandfather's life. Following in this tradition both John Upton and his son Richard became significant figures in racehorse training and bookmaking, and were known in the racing world as Jock and Dickie. Richard, or Dickie, suffered severely from asthma, and this affected his schooling and meant he could not join the army. He married Susan Lendrum, née Charrington, who had two children by her first marriage. She and Richard had a daughter, Matilda Frances Upton, and a son, Richard Francis Upton. The names of both these children illustrate the continuity of a naming tradition that, in the case of Francis, goes back for 300 years at least, and in the case of Upton, to the marriage of Thomas Gaskell to Mary Upton in 1773.

Whilst descendants of the Gaskells (on both the Gaskell and the Pawson side) still survive, living mainly in the London area, the connection with Ingersley was severed many years ago. It would seem that after the death of John Francis in 1929 there must have been some discussion as to the best course of action to take. The 1920s and 30s were of course a period of recession in this country, but it was also a time when grand country houses were proving expensive to maintain and difficult to staff, and moreover, the notion of a lord of the manor was becoming outdated. In the Gaskells' case, there was also the consideration that their lives were now based far from the north of England and increasingly at a remove from the way of life of the landed gentry. In particular, John Upton's focus was very much on training his racehorses from his then home at Exeter House in Newmarket, and he had no real use for Ingersley. Hence in 1933 the decision was taken to sell the Ingersley estate. One or two of the farms were bought by the existing tenants, but the Hall, the rest of the farms, two cottages near Rainow Mill, the land and houses in Rainow and Bollington, and the reservoir in Ingersley Road were divided into lots to be sold by auction at the Angel Hotel in Macclesfield on 20th June 1933. Ingersley Hall and Farm were, however, withdrawn from the auction and sold privately.

The week before, the sale of the contents of Ingersley Hall had begun. The sale was held at the Hall itself and took six days. A report of the hundreds of lots sold, together with their prices, was available for all to see in the local newspaper *The Macclesfield Courier*.[47] The auction encompassed an eclectic range of articles: from an Elizabethan dining table to a 'genuine' man trap; from the finest of miniatures to a hair mattress; from a 'very fine' racoon skin rug with 24 tails to a warming pan; and from blue silk curtains 'over 100 years old with condition and colouring equal to new' to 30 volumes of Dickens. Many quality pieces were included, such as Sheraton, Hepplewhite and Chippendale furniture, and Worcester, Dresden, Sèvres and Crown Derby china. These, not surprisingly, achieved the higher prices. Amongst the items sold were the pictures John Upton Gaskell had bought in 1857 at Alton Towers and which had belonged to Letitia Bonaparte. One of these was the painting thought to be of Archimedes which sold for just £7, considerably less than John Upton had paid for it. The marble statue of Marie Antoinette which the Gaskells had bought in Paris achieved only £1, a fairly average price for many of the smaller items. There were many antiques featured in the sale, some of which must have been considered to be family heirlooms.

A section of the Plan produced for the Sale of the Ingersley estate in 1933, showing the various lots. The words 'Lot 9' in the centre are set in the walled kitchen garden.

One example was a:

> magnificent old oak Elizabethan bedstead with 3 small carved panels in footboard and carved top rail with Tudor Rose and dragons, carved head with 3 arched panels, carved and inlaid with satinwood floral design, initialled LB 1528, having canopy top with 8 plain and one carved panel supported by two heavily carved panels from footboard.

It is not inconceivable that bearing the initial B this had belonged to the Brocklehursts, who were an important family as early as the sixteenth century when such elaborate beds were only possessed by the wealthy. More easily attributable are an old oak chest initialled JG 1667, and another chest with carved panels and top rail engraved John Gesskill. The former is almost certainly the chest left in 1701 by John Gaskell of Handley to his grandson John of Adlington, whilst the latter was probably even older, given the spelling of the surname.

Ingersley Hall itself was bought by Edward Lomas, a silk manufacturer and Catholic benefactor from Macclesfield. He did not intend to live at Ingersley himself but to allow it to be used by the Sisters of Notre Dame of Manchester as a holiday centre. He instigated a comprehensive renovation and redecoration programme which was still underway when, on 6th March 1937, a drastic fire broke out. A farmer who lived a mile away was tending his cattle in the early hours of the morning when he saw a glow in the sky. Realising what it must mean he ran through snow to raise the tenants of Ingersley Farm, adjacent to the Hall. This was in the days before telephones and a car had to be sent down to Bollington Police Station to alert the fire service. By the time they arrived the fire had broken through the roof and flames were rising into the sky. It seemed impossible to save that part of the building, and efforts were directed at preventing any further spread with water pumped from nearby trout ponds. The damage was extensive:

> What had been the beautiful old entrance hall [was] a mass of charred wreckage. The central staircase which had been one of the attractions of the hall was simply a mass of twisted iron. The drawing and dining rooms either side of the central hall, and overlooking Kerridge hills on one side and the old English parkland on the other was [sic] ruined, the dining room in particular. The bedrooms above them were gutted, only the walls and charred beams remaining. The roof and attics immediately above the main entrance were also ruined and so great was the damage that it is believed that the outbreak commenced in that portion of the building. . . . The library which adjoined the drawing room, was badly damaged by water.[48]

After the fire the Hall was repaired and for a few years was used as planned for the Sisters of Notre Dame. However the idea was eventually proposed that it should be taken on as additional accommodation for the Catholic order of the Salesians of Don Bosco, with whom Mr Lomas was also associated. The Salesians ran a missionary school and college at Shrigley Hall a few miles away, and an influx of students after the war meant that they were short of space. So in 1952 the Salesians bought Ingersley Hall, promptly changing its name to Savio House in honour of the famous pupil St Dominic Savio, who died in Turin aged 15, and who was sanctified for his piety and compassion. Today, after the eventual closure of the facilities at Shrigley Hall and a period during which the fortunes of the Salesians have ebbed and flowed, Savio House is run as a retreat and conference centre for young people.

Ingersley Hall today, now Savio House

Over the years much work has been done both inside and out to make the Hall suitable for the Salesians' needs. This included initially making the building weather tight and installing an electricity supply to replace the existing gas lighting. Inside, various rooms were reshaped for new purposes, including a first floor chapel. A few years later a brick extension was built to the rear of the house to provide a new kitchen and more bedrooms above, and the outbuildings were also considerably altered, some in the 1950s (before the buildings were listed in 1967 and hence not always sympathetically), and some later. For example the conservatory near the south door was demolished; the archway to the coach house was filled in and dormitories created; the stable block and cow byres became meeting rooms with sleeping accommodation above; the dovecot and pig sty were turned into living accommodation; and, most recently, a new games room was added as an extension to the coach house.

The old farmhouse was very much at the centre of these outbuildings and until 1970 it continued to be operated as a farm under the then tenants, the Nadens. Then the farmhouse too was turned into additional accommodation. The Salesians themselves were not involved in farming, nor did they have any interest in the walled garden. This remained abandoned until the 1970s when one of the lay employees began to re-create a productive kitchen garden. However the initiative did not last and it then lay neglected until it was offered to a group of community gardeners in recent years. Meanwhile the old trout pond which lay near the house just outside the kitchen garden was filled in to create a car park and the grounds nearest to the house were gradually adapted for service use or recreational areas.

The view over former Gaskell land from the driveway across the parkland and Ingersley Vale to White Nancy. The chimney stack of Ingersley Vale Mill is just visible on the right.

The period since the Gaskells lived at Ingersley has thus been a time of considerable change, and what was once a home has become an institution. Sadly, this has meant that the names of both the Gaskells and of Ingersley Hall are beginning to fade from local consciousness. The Hall itself still stands, however it is now referred to as 'Savio', and associated not with a resident squire but with a congregation of people seen by many as belonging to a somewhat remote religious order. It is not open to the public, but the glimpses that can be caught from the footpaths that cross from Oakenbank Lane to Ingersley Vale suggest to passers-by that its essential character, externally at least, remains. Indeed, it is this character which has led to its listing as a building of national importance.

The Gaskells themselves have become little more than shadowy figures, dimly recalled from the memories and tales of a previous generation. Yet in their time they were a noteworthy family, not only because of their contribution to local life and their generosity, but as an example of how, with determination and a degree of opportunism, it was possible to rise from a position of relative servitude to become prosperous and join the ranks of the landed gentry.

The family may indeed be long gone, but their influence lives on in the surrounding landscape. For it is the acquisition, shaping, and use of the land which have resulted in the heritage so appreciated by residents and visitors alike. This heritage reveals itself as a rich tapestry made up of many interwoven strands: fields; stone walls; flagged paths; hedgerows; farmhouses; stands of trees; industrial remains; pools; bridges; and water courses. Most prominent of all, of course, is that iconic landmark we know as White Nancy. Conceived by the Gaskells, it stands as proudly now as it did 200 years ago, an enduring monument to the individuals who themselves once walked and rested here.

Notes and References

[1] The derivation of Gatesgill is from the Norse *gait* for goat or *Geiti* a personal name, and *scale* for shieling, hut or shelter. Gaisgil stems from the old Scandinavian *gais* goose and *gil* ravine or deep valley. See Sedgefield, Walter John (1915, reprinted 2013) *The Place-Names of Cumberland and Westmoreland* London, Forgotten Books.

[2] See http://www.surnamedb.com.

[3] The area granted to the Leghs was nominally divided into Lyme, the wooded area to the north and west and later the location of the house and park, and Handley, also spelt Hanley, the pasturage to the south and east, but as a township eventually the whole area became known as Lyme Handley.

[4] For histories of the Leghs and Lyme see Beamont W. (1876) *A History of the House of Lyme* P. Pease, Warrington, and Newton, Lady (1917) *The House of Lyme from its Foundations to the End of the Eighteenth Century* Heinemann, London.

[5] Tonkinson A.M. (1999) *Macclesfield in the Later Fourteenth Century: Communities of Town and Forest*, Chetham Society, Manchester, and Tonkinson A. M. (1990) *A List of Individuals Appearing in the Halmote and Portmote Courts of Macclesfield in the second half of the Fourteenth Century*, Mimeo.

[6] Fothergill J and B and Ranulf Higden Society (2011) *The Legh of Lyme Survey Compiled by Sir Peter Legh of Lyme and Bradley*, Ranulf Higden Society.

[7] Ormerod George (1882, revised edition) *The History of the County Palatine and City of Chester*, George Helsby.

[8] Geneaological information throughout is drawn from http://www.ancestry.co.uk, http://www.findmypast.co.uk, http://www.familysearch.org, memorial inscriptions, censuses, http://www.disley.net, and wills.

[9] The Star Chamber courts were held at the Palace of Westminster and concerned matters such as corruption, riots, public disorder, and property rights.

[10] Stewart-Brown, R. (1816) *Lancashire and Cheshire Cases in the Court of Star Chamber Part 1*, The Record Society (available online) p.93, p.131 and p.134.

[11] Newton, Lady (ibid), p.60.

[12] *Legh of Lyme Muniments Correspondence*, Boxes 1 and 3, John Rylands Library.

[13] *1686 Survey*, Legh of Lyme Muniments Box Q, John Rylands Library.

[14] *Sacrament Certificates*, QSJ/8/19/220, Lancashire Archives.

[15] I am indebted to Tom Swailes for sourcing this information from the private archive collection of the Leghs of Adlington Hall.

[16] *Downes Deeds 1288-1866*, DDS/441, DDS/454, DDS/473, DDS/475, Cheshire Record Office.

[17] Ingersley was an ancient settlement dating from at least the early fourteenth century, with the name deriving from the Norse Ingaldslegh, Ingald being a personal name and 'legh' a clearing. See Laughton, Jane (1990) *Seventeenth Century Rainow: The Story of a Cheshire Hill Village*.

[18] This is probably the valuable antiquarian Bible *The Holy Bible, conteining the Olde Testament and the Newe*, with family records inscribed: 'among those mentioned are John son of John and Ellen Gaskell of Adlington born 18th November 1717, and Peter Gaskell of Ingersley', listed for sale for a four figure sum by AbeBooks in 2013.

[19] Copyhold was a form of tenure dating from the fifteenth century whereby land was held under a lord of the manor and could be inherited by a next of kin, or was held for 'three lives' so that two successors could be nominated to inherit after the death of the first. Various nineteenth century Copyhold Acts converted this form of tenure to freehold or 999 year leasehold, and in 1926 all copyhold land finally became freehold.

[20] Simm, George (1996) *The Life and Times of Peter Legh the Younger*, Willow Printing, Newton le Willows p.63.

[21] Rainow Women's Institute (undated) *The Story of Rainow*.

[22] *Legh of Lyme Muniments*, Box Q, E, No15, John Rylands Library; *Legh Family of Lyme Hall*, E/17/90/ 2 and 3, Manchester Central Library.

[23] Stancliffe F.S. (1938) *John Shaw's 1738-1938*, Sherratt and Hughes, Timperley.

[24] *Legh of Lyme Muniments* Box Q, E, No 15, John Rylands Library.

[25] Longden, George (2002) *Kerridge Ridge and Ingersley Vale: A Historical Study*, KRIV Heritage Project.

[26] Longden (ibid).

[27] For information on local mills see Kerridge Ridge and Ingersley Vale Countryside and Heritage Project (2009) *A Landscape History*, and Calladine, Anthony and Fricker, Jean (1993) *East Cheshire Textile Mills*, RCHM, London.

[28] Langton, Richard (1836) *Narrative of a Captivity in France 1800-1816* Vol 1, Smith, Elder and Co, Cornhill pp. 157-162.

[29] See Longden (ibid), Kelly's (1878) *Post Office Directory of Cheshire*, Bollington Festival Committee (1980) *When Nancy was Young*, Marriott, Rev William (1810) *The Antiquities of Lyme and its Vicinity*.

[30] Smith, Walter (1948) *Notes on White Nancy*, Macclesfield Courier, March 25th.

[31] *UK Poll Books and Electoral Registers*, 1538-1893, available on http://www.ancestry.co.uk.

[32] Longden (ibid).

[33] The mill was over time leased to various people and became famous for having the second largest water wheel in Britain, installed about 1850. It continued in operation long after the Gaskells had left Ingersley and was used for a variety of purposes until a fire in 1999 ended all activity. It has since been the subject of various

development proposals, none of which has so far been implemented, and after much demolition only the facade remains.

[34] Ashby, Abby and Jones, Audrey (2003) *The Shrigley Abduction*, Sutton Publishing.

[35] *Letters from John Upton Gaskell to his Parents*, 1824-1830, DDX462, Cheshire Record Office.

[36] For more information on the Grimshawes and Errwood Hall see http://.www.goyt-valley.org.uk.

[37] *The Manchester Courier and Lancashire General Advertiser* 21st March 1874.

[38] It was sold in 2012 at Christies in London for £58,850, see *Derby Daily Telegraph* 24 March 1938, and http://www.christies.com.

[39] *Chester Chronicle*, 29th September 1855 p.6.

[40] *Derbyshire Advertiser and Journal* 16th December, 1870.

[41] I am grateful to Tom Swailes for a transcript of the witness statement. Further information can be found at http://www.parliament.uk/business/publications.

[42] *Macclesfield Courier*, 11th August 1883 p.5.

[43] *Sandhurst News Letter*, 30th June 1870 p.1.

[44] *Macclesfield Courier*, 20th January 1894 p.8.

[45] See also Rainow History Group (2006) *Rainow Caught in Time: Images of an Upland Village*, Rainow History Group.

[46] *Macclesfield Courier*, 14th April 1923 p.10.

[47] *Macclesfield Courier*, 23rd June 1933 p.6.

[48] *Macclesfield Courier*, 12th March 1937 p.3.